A Student Commentary on Plato's Euthyphro

MICHIGAN CLASSICAL COMMENTARIES

Patrick Paul Hogan
    A Student Commentary on Pausanius Book 1

Celia E. Schultz
    A Commentary on Cicero, *De Divinatione I*

Erin K. Moodie
    Plautus' *Poenulus*: A Student Commentary

Donka D. Markus
    Reading Medieval Latin with the Legend of Barlaam and Josaphat

Patrick Paul Hogan
    A Student Commentary on Pausanius Book 2

Charles Platter
    A Student Commentary on Plato's *Euthyphro*

A Student Commentary on Plato's *Euthyphro*

Charles Platter

University of Michigan Press
Ann Arbor

Published in the United States of America by the
University of Michigan Press
Manufactured in the United States of America
Printed on acid-free paper

A CIP catalog record for this book is available from the British Library.

Library of Congress Cataloging-in-Publication data has been applied for.

First published October 2019

ISBN: 978-0-472-07432-7 (Hardcover : alk paper)
ISBN: 978-0-472-05432-9 (Paper : alk paper)

Acknowledgments

The pleasure of working on this commentary has been augmented by the help and indulgence I have received on the way. Colleagues at the University of Georgia, especially Christine Albright, Thomas Biggs, Benjamin Wolkow, and departmental exegete Peter O'Connell, have been generous with their learning. Suzanne Jurado provided important assistance checking references and proofreading. Mary Hashman from the University of Michigan Press did a superb job of copyediting a challenging manuscript. Thanks also to Ellen Baurle, whose support, advice, and good humor have been essential at all stages of this project.

Stephen Fineberg of Knox College graciously supplied me with the manuscript of a *Euthyphro* commentary written by himself and Jonathan Lee which was extremely useful. Thanks to both of them for their acuity and willingness to share! In 2009 I had the good fortune to attend a Classical Commentary Workshop at Georgetown run by S. Douglas Olson and Alexander Sens. Thanks to both of them and the rest of the writing group for their attention to detail and good sense in thinking about the goals of commentary-writing. Thanks also to Paul Allen Miller, my collaborator for Plato's *Apology of Socrates: A Commentary*. The approaches we developed for that project also were essential for writing on the *Euthyphro*.

I was able to use a preliminary version of the commentary with a graduate seminar on the *Euthyphro* at the University of Georgia in the spring of 2018 and benefited from the comments of those students. I gave Euthyphro presentations at CAMWS-Southern Section and the Society for Comparative Literature and the Arts along the way and profited from those discussions. Other captive audiences, my daughters Clara Platter and Louise Platter, also gave important editorial and philosophical input.

I tried to learn Greek as an undergraduate at Grinnell College. Although my efforts were insufficient—much had to be relearned later—we spent the last half of the second semester reading Plato's *Apology of Socrates* out of A.M. Adams' little yellow student commentary. We had to memorize passages in those days;

for this class the text was *Apology* 29a-b, where Socrates contrasts the ignorant assumptions that undergird our fear of death with the certainty that it is wrong to act in a way that you know is shameful (cf. *Euthphr.* 12b-c). I got to know the passage well in memorizing it and so understood it more accurately than much of the text. I was struck by the first line, τὸ γάρ τοι θάνατον δεδιέναι, ὦ ἄνδρες, οὐδὲν ἄλλο εστὶν ἢ δοκεῖν σοφὸν εἶναι, μὴ ὄντα, particularly the pithy μὴ ὄντα, which negates the unjustified claims to wisdom that many people make. You could say truly that it was the first Greek sentence I felt I understood. I tell my elementary Greek students that their persistence, too, will be rewarded, that there will be a moment when they encounter a sentence of a certain difficulty the meaning of which will be crystal clear, that this epiphany will occur sooner rather than later, and that it will make all their struggles to learn Greek seem to have been worth it. In the spirit of this hope, this commentary is dedicated to them.

Contents

Introduction

It is rare for the same person to be a great writer and an important philosopher. As both, Plato is even more remarkable for the fact that he sits at the beginning of the Western philosophical tradition. It is true that thinkers before him presented their thoughts in both written and oral conversations. The most obvious example among them is Socrates, who wrote nothing himself. Pre-Socratic philosophers who wrote on a broad range of topics include Thales, Heraclitus, Anaximander, Parmenides, Xeno, and Anaxagoras, to name a few.[1] Still, the weight of the tradition that Plato inherited from his predecessors was substantially lighter than the one he bequeathed to his successors. That imbalance is both a blessing and a curse. It is a curse in that Plato virtually had to invent many of the philosophical issues that his successors have taken for granted. Yet his position at the beginning of the tradition allowed him to compose without being constrained by the imposing shadow of a great predecessor. In this sense, then, the work of Plato represents the lucky arrival of a great original talent at the perfect time and place. The result is a body of work that addresses issues important both to fourth-century Athenians and to inhabitants of the twenty-first century.

This modernity claim may not seem so obviously true for *Euthyphro*. For many, the mention of piety will conjure up visions of fundamentalist sects eager to impose their beliefs on others. If *Euthyphro* were created in the same spirit of moral certainty, we might rightly question its ability to speak to important contemporary concerns across a broad spectrum of readers. However, the dialogue goes in the opposite direction. Socrates' interlocutor, Euthyphro, if not a zealot, is a man perfectly confident in his ability to know and say which actions are or are not holy. Precisely that conviction has brought him to Athens to charge his father with murder for indifferently allowing the death of an employee. From a fifth-century perspective, according to which paternal obedience was expected of all sons, Euthyphro's actions are shocking. Yet Plato

---

1. For the fragments (with English translation), see Kirk, Raven, and Schofield 1983.

takes pains to make them seem less so. The father's actions are described in such a way that their callousness comes through loud and clear; he will deserve any punishment he gets.

Whatever we may think of the father, it is Euthyphro who is at the center of the dialogue. Moreover, the subject of Socrates' scrutiny is less Euthyphro's actions themselves than his moral certainty, which Socrates suspects is not justified and which shows no signs of having been acquired through any deep meditation on the nature of right and wrong. Readers from the twenty-first century may see many parallels between the intellectual laziness of Euthyphro and the style of discourse that characterizes much of contemporary life. For a world that often seems exhausted before the powers of unreason, then, Socrates' decision to expose Euthyphro's pretenses should be uplifting. The piety that emerges from the conversation between these men is uncertain in many respects. It may reject traditional religious dogma, if it is true that different gods love and hate different things. Without equivocation, however, it rejects moral assertions based only on tradition or authority and insists that our actions should be the result of active reasoning. In this sense, therefore, few Platonic dialogues are as relevant to the historical period in which we find ourselves.

Life of Plato

The biography of Plato is difficult to write with confidence. A group of thirteen letters survive, although the authenticity of many has been doubted.[2] The dialogues fill five large volumes in the Oxford Classical Texts series, but they have little to say specifically about Plato.[3] Finally, many of the large number of extant anecdotes are not believable. Ancient biography is frequently partisan, as both hagiography and invective. Some authors draw liberally from both traditions. We hear from Diogenes Laertius, for example, that the "divine" Plato was born on the same day as Apollo (hagiography) and that Socrates maligned the dialogues as nothing but lies (invective).[4] In presenting the life of Plato, I often rely on the account of Diogenes Laertius but attempt to steer in the direction of the parts where a reasonable scholarly consensus exists. I have also

---

2. The only letter that figures in the account given here is the seventh. For a discussion of the letters, see Guthrie 1978, 399–417.

3. After his conviction, Socrates refers to Plato in the *Apology*, as one member of a group of friends who have offered to pay a fine on his behalf (38b7). In addition, Phaedo, narrator of the dialogue of the same name, lists Plato as someone not present, because of an illness, at the death of Socrates (59b10).

4. D.L. 3.2, 36. For a study of the anecdotal tradition, see Riginos 1976.

included passages from the *Seventh Letter*, which many assume to be authentic or at least based on good sources.[5]

Plato (ca. 428–348 BCE) was born into a prominent Athenian family. His mother, Perictione, traced her descent to Solon and, back still further, to the god Poseidon. Her husband, Ariston, was a descendant of Codrus, a legendary king of Athens *also* supposedly related to Poseidon (D.L. 3.1–2). After Ariston's death, Perictione married her uncle Pyrilampes, who was a friend of Pericles and frequently served as an Athenian ambassador (see Nails 2002, 257–59, for a summary of the sources for Pyrilampes).

Many of Plato's relatives were prominent critics of the Athenian democracy. His cousin Critias (*PA* 8792; Nails 2002, 108–11) and uncle Charmides (*PA* 15512; Nails 2002, 90–94) were prominent members of the Thirty, a group of oligarchs who rose to power briefly in the wake of the Spartan victory in the Peloponnesian War (404–403). Critias was their leader, and Charmides was one of the Ten, a group of commissioners in charge of activities in the Piraeus. Both were killed at the Battle of Munychia in 403 BCE by the forces of the exiled democrats under Thrasybulus (X. *Hell.* 2.4.19).

Although invited to participate in the government of the Thirty, Plato chose to wait and observe—fortunately, as he notes in the *Seventh Letter*:

> Some of these men happened to be family members and acquaintances of mine. Right away they invited me to be a part of the new state. Given my youth, it was unsurprising that I thought they would manage the city and lead it from an unjust life to a just one. Thus, I paid particular attention to what they would do. But I quickly watched them demonstrate by their actions that the previous government was like the Golden Age. (324d)

Plato particularly notes the attempt of the Thirty to implicate Socrates ("the most just man alive") by ordering him to arrest Leon, a prominent Athenian general who would be executed notoriously by the Thirty (324e). For the arrest and execution of Leon, see Andoc. 1.94; Lys. 10.4; *Ap.* 32c1 (unless otherwise noted, citations of the *Apology* refer to Plato's *Apology of Socrates*); Lys.13.44 probably also alludes to Leon. Such incidents were not isolated acts. As a result, Plato did not cooperate with the government, which fell soon afterward (*Seventh Letter* 325a).

Nothing about Plato's activities at this time is known. Though there is no record of his military service, a man of his high social class would have served in the cavalry. He is presumed to have remained in the city rather

---

5. For a recent negative assessment of the letter's authenticity, see Burnyeat and Frede 2015.

than to have joined the democratic faction in exile at Phyle. For a family like Plato's, that choice could have been read as signaling support for the oligarchy. Nevertheless, there is no indication of reprisals against him after the restoration of the democracy, and he is represented in the *Apology* as present at the trial of Socrates (38b7). Thus, Plato's presumed political affiliations did not seem to have serious consequences for him after the Thirty fell.

According to Plato, the restored democrats behaved with considerable moderation—except in one instance.

> Unfortunately, however, the men in power brought my friend Socrates into court, claiming the most unholy and proposterous accusation possible. For they brought him to trial for impiety, convicted, and executed him. (325)

Socrates was accused of *asebeia* (*impiety*), particularly for neglecting the traditional practices of Athenian religion and introducing new gods.[6] The accusers said that in so doing, Socrates corrupted the youth with whom he associated.

Much about the case is unclear. Many have speculated that Socrates was prosecuted to satisfy a desire for revenge among the restored democrats, who saw him as a supporter of Critias and the notorious Alcibiades.[7] Moreover, the resolution of the civil war brokered by the Spartan general Pausanias included an amnesty provision that extended to all but the Thirty and their closest allies (*Ath.* 39; Rhodes 1993). As a result, those whose fortunes were confiscated or whose relatives were murdered may have been unable to take revenge directly on the perpetrators. Some people may have felt that their only opportunity was to attack an enemy indirectly by beginning legal proceedings against a friend of someone protected by the amnesty. It is possible, therefore, that the impiety charge was such a pretext for political revenge against the associates of Socrates, if not against the man himself.[8]

---

6. For versions of the indictment, see Xen. *Ap.* 1.10–11; D.L. 2.40; Plato, *Ap.* 24b8–c1. See also Xen. *Mem.* 1.2.9: "But the accuser [probably the composer of a later essay purporting to represent a prosecutor at the actual trial] said, 'By Zeus, he caused his companions to despise established laws, saying that it is stupid to choose by lot the rulers of the city, and that no one would be willing to use that method to choose the captain of a ship, a carpenter, or a flute player.'"

7. Whether or not this sentiment was a major factor, the idea possessed durability. Xenophon addressed the issue at length at *Mem.* 1.2.12–48. Half a century later, the orator Aeschines used the supposed effect of Socrates on Critias as a parallel for the corrosive effects of his rival Demosthenes (*Ti.* 173). For a recent assessment of the impiety charge, see Ralkowski 2013.

8. Carawan (2013, 212–16) argues that the *asebeia* charge was the most important part of the case against Socrates but that it was connected directly with the association between Socrates and Critias.

The Socratic writings about the trial give no clear indication that Socrates was a political target. In Plato's *Apology, Socrates* denies that he is anyone's teacher and points, in his defense, to his willingness to defy the Thirty by refusing to arrest Leon of Salamis. He does address the charge of *asebeia* quite directly, however, as does the *Apology* of Xenophon (11), which, in turn, claims to be derived from the work of Plato's pupil Hermogenes.[9] More important, neither Plato in the *Seventh Letter* nor Xenophon in the *Apology* and *Memorabilia* imply that there was a political conspiracy.[10]

Two events in Plato's life are fairly well documented and require special mention. The first is a series of visits to Syracuse in Sicily, which caused him to become entangled in the cutthroat world of politics at the courts of the tyrants Dionysius I and Dionysius II. The second is the foundation of the Academy, which became a significant center of learning in Athens and would continue to be an important institution for nearly three hundred years. Around 387, at the age of forty, Plato made a visit to Italy, perhaps desiring to meet the Pythagorean philosopher-statesman Archytus of Tarentum. For reasons that he does not explain, Plato also went to Syracuse in Sicily, where he was invited to the court of the tyrant Dionysius I (c. 432–367 BCE) and met one of that tyrant's ministers, Dion (c. 408–354 BCE), with whom Plato shared a close friendship for over thirty years. Plato's relationship with Dionysius was less enduring. After having spoken too freely to Dionysius on his ideas about government, Plato is said to have been sold into slavery by him and was only able to return to Athens after having been ransomed by friends. That story is not mentioned in the Platonic letters and may have been created by Plato's rivals to discredit him. Nevertheless, he did not return to Syracuse while Dionysius I lived.

It seems most likely that one of Plato's primary activities on returning to Athens was the creation of the Academy, a center of study that attracted students from across the Greek world and became the model of educational fellowship. Plato's school took its name from its location in a suburb of Athens, near a grove sacred to the hero Academus.[11] Plato lived and taught as the *scholarch* of the Academy for the rest of his life. Many details of the administration and curriculum of the Academy are uncertain. Mathematics were likely to have figured significantly, as well as astronomy and political theory. Plato was joined at the Academy by many important intellectual figures of his time. Aristotle

---

9. The charge is also implied by the remarks of Xenophon at *Mem.* 1.2. For further discussion, see the commentary herein on *Euthphr.* 3b3.

10. Omitting reference to such matters might be understandable, both for Plato, who continued to live in Athens under the restored democracy, and for Xenophon, who lived in Olympia and Corinth but maintained Athenian connections. Nevertheless, an argument from silence is hardly conclusive.

11. *Th.* 2.34. For a discussion of the school and its topography, see Baltes 1993; Watts 2007.

spent twenty years there. The mathematician Eudoxus of Cnidus was also a member, as was Plato's nephew and first successor, Speusippus. The Academy continued to thrive after the death of Plato, until it was destroyed by Sulla in 86 BCE, during the First Mithridatic War (Plu. *Sull.* 12.3).

Despite his better judgment, Plato returned to Syracuse twenty years after his initial visit. Dionysius II had succeeded his father as tyrant. Dion said that the young ruler had philosophical aspirations and, as the story goes, access to Dionysius II via Dion offered Plato an opportunity to attempt to put his ideas about government into practice. The court of Dionysius II (c. 397–343 BCE) was thick with intrigue, however. Dion's enemies were many. They probably would have seen Plato as Dion's ally in the struggle for power and influence and would have lost no opportunity to frustrate and discredit both men. Soon after Plato's arrival, Dion was accused of conspiracy and exiled. Meanwhile, Dionysius II, swayed by his courtiers and his natural inclinations, showed no interest in giving his attention to philosophy. Plato returned to Athens around 365. He was persuaded to come to Sicily once more in 361, by recommendations from Archytas of Tarentum that Dionysius II was now serious about philosophy. Nothing had changed, however. Plato remarks ruefully that he was lucky to have escaped that visit with his life. After a short time, he returned to Athens and the Academy, where he spent the remaining years before his death in 348.

The Platonic Dialogue

Since everyone knows that Plato wrote dialogues—and only dialogues, for the most part—it can be easy to overlook the fact that the dialogue is not the most obvious vehicle for philosophical thought. Philosophers since Plato typically have not employed it, except those self-consciously emulating him (one immediately thinks of Cicero in this regard). The reason for avoiding dialogue is not hard to see. If I want to communicate an idea, I begin by thinking carefully about what I want to argue. If the point is complicated, I need to break it down into its constituent parts, decide what evidence is relevant for each part, present that evidence, and draw the appropriate conclusions. If I follow that template, I end up with an essay. If I do the same on a greater scale, I have a book. In writing either an essay or a book, I would work carefully to define the topic and rigorously edit out material that does not contribute to the general thesis for which I want to argue. Finally, as the author of the essay or book, I am also its narrator. The opinions expressed are my own, and what I say goes. The reader has no reason to doubt that I mean what I say. A dialogue is utterly different. By adding characters, the author—if there is one—makes it unclear how to interpret the conversation. Do the speakers agree or disagree, find common ground or become increasingly hostile? How can we know which (if any) of the expressed points of view represents the view of the author? These and many other questions present themselves to the reader of a Platonic dialogue and thus distinguish reading one from reading a philosophical treatise. In preparing to read *Euthyphro*, then, we need to consider Plato's rejection of the essay for communicating his ideas. How does embedding them in dialogue affect our interpretation of his work?

We may begin to address that question by appealing to the cultural context within which Plato wrote. In the fifth and fourth centuries, Greece was still very much an oral and performative culture. The private possession of books was sufficiently common for Socrates to mention, in the *Apology*, that the "book" of Anaxagoras could be purchased cheaply in the agora (26d). Still, the most common means of encountering the ideas of others was as part of a live performance or conversation. In symposia, at dramatic and musical performances, in the assembly, and in the law courts, participants spoke directly to an audience that often spoke back to them. Practitioners of wisdom, too—philosophers, sophists, healers, interpreters of dreams, and others—competed for attention in the public forums of every sort.[12] In such a world, it is not surprising that one's assumptions about the dissemination of ideas would incline toward those that most closely mimic the conditions of actual speech. Writing is an unproven technology in such a climate. Clearly, it can preserve thought. Still, it lacks the flexibility of a conversation, in which the participants adjust what they say to anticipate the attitudes or interests of their conversational partners, then either refine their meaning in the face of objections or concede all or part of their argument.

This bias against writing is perceivable in Plato's *Phaedrus*, where Socrates tells a story about the Egyptian god Theuth, the inventor of writing, who brings his discovery to King Thamus and explains that it will make the Egyptians wiser and improve their memories (274e). Thamus is not impressed and says that if humans rely on external marks (writing) rather than wisdom that is within themselves, they will become more forgetful, not less (275a). From this story, Socrates concludes that "anyone who leaves behind a written treatise, and anyone who receives it, thinking that on account of the writing it will be safe and secure, would be very simpleminded" (275c). Thus, we see in *Phaedrus* the same trust in the superiority of live, interactive conversation that was a feature of Greek society of the fifth and fourth centuries as a whole. Although we cannot say certainly that Plato shared Socrates' attitude toward writing, the language of the *Seventh Letter* suggests that he did. In discussing the report that

---

12. See, for example, Tell 2007, which documents and discusses the "intellectual displays" of wisdom by sages at athletic competitions.

Dionysius II has composed a treatise (*techne*) summarizing his doctrines, Plato denies that such a thing could exist and says that philosophical enlightenment appears not as the result of a book but like a flame kindled by a spark after great communal effort (*ek polles sunousias*, 341c).

The Platonic dialogues express traditional Greek beliefs about the superiority of spoken words to written ones. As we have seen, this bias is corroborated by Plato in the *Seventh Letter*. The agreement between these sources could be taken as confirmation that the bias is Plato's personal opinion also. Yet it is not easy to square this attitude with the fact that Plato was a prolific writer whose works in translation amount to over fifteen hundred pages. Plato does not tell us how to sort out this problem. Perhaps, as Leo Strauss suggests (1966, 52), Plato saw the dialogue as the type of writing most free from its essential defect. In any case, it will be useful to consider briefly what is at stake when an author like Plato turns to the dialogue form.

Richard Kraut's summary may be a good place from which to begin.

> The best way to form a reasonable conjecture about why Plato wrote any given work in the form of a dialogue is to ask: what would be lost, were one to attempt to rewrite this work in a way that eliminated the give-and-take of interchange, stripped the characters of their personality and social markers, and transformed the result into something that comes straight from the mouth of the author?[13]

The variety of the Platonic dialogues is so great that no single approach will answer Kraut's question adequately. In addition, to survey the different ways this question would have to be answered in regard to each dialogue would be a mammoth undertaking. I continue, then, by applying Kraut's question to *Euthyphro*, where it will become clear quickly that the dialogue form is essential to this work.

The primary subject of *Euthyphro* is piety (*to hosion*, literally, "the holy"). The work includes a substantial introduction, which explains how Euthyphro and Socrates came to be in the same place at the same time, a boast by Euthyphro that he is an expert on piety, a request by Socrates for a definition of piety, and several unsuccessful attempts by Euthyphro to provide one. The dialogue ends without a solution to the problem, thus identifying *Euthyphro* as *aporetic* (i.e., ending in *aporia*, "perplexity," rather than reaching positive conclusions). Since the dialogue does not conclusively define piety, everything that is important about the work must be derived from the different types of exchanges between Socrates and Euthyphro. To translate this statement into Kraut's terms, if

---

13. Kraut 2017.

Euthyphro were rewritten as a treatise, much of the dialogue would disappear. This claim should not be taken to imply that there is no positive content to the dialogue; instead, it affirms that the tentative answers considered explicitly or implied by the participants, together with the "give-and-take of interchange," force readers to think through the issues in play for themselves, without having the conclusions predigested for them by an author or a teacher. The relationship between the answers considered and the interchange between the participants is therefore critical to the implicit pedagogy of Platonic writing.

This linkage between Socrates and Euthyphro illustrates well how the details of the dramatic presentation affect the content of the dialogue. As we shall see, both Euthyphro and Socrates are present at the Royal Stoa for reasons that are explicitly linked with piety. Both Euthyphro's definition of piety as that which is beloved by the gods and the alterations made to that definition in the course of the dialogue serve to point at, but not explicitly to argue for, the idea that *to hosion* can only be meaningful as a part of the Good, regardless of what the gods think about it. Thus, the form of the dialogue is not merely decorative; in fact, Plato allows it to be the primary carrier of meaning within the work.

Such an approach to *Euthyphro* leads us to further questions. Granted that the dialogue form is crucial for *Euthyphro*, why did Plato write this dialogue at all? If he wanted to argue that the ethical decisions that people make should be analyzed according to how the decisions fit into the cosmic idea of the Good, why did he not just write a treatise called *On the Good* and leave it at that?

As has been already argued, Plato's dialogues have a pedagogical orientation; that is, they are designed to simulate the process of coming to a conclusion organically (*ek polles sunousias*, as he says in the *Seventh Letter*). In *Phaedrus*, Socrates complains that books say the same thing to all who possess them, whether those readers are clever or dull, thoughtful or reckless (275d–e). Certainly, as noted earlier, an essay or a treatise works on this principle: the author/narrator proposes a topic, establishes the context for the topic, sets out what thesis will be argued, and rejects or omits topics that will not be covered. Throughout the work, then, we are going to be listening to the same voice, who will be telling us how to think. The author may be truly brilliant, the subject matter challenging, and the argument utterly compelling. The opposite also may be true, as well as every possibility in between. In any case, readers are asked to begin by acknowledging the authority of the narrator and to subordinate their perspectives to that of the writer.

Of course, the exemplary character of Socrates dominates most of the dialogues, although it is not a simple matter to determine whether the arguments advanced are those of the historical Socrates, who died when Plato was still in his twenties, or Plato's. It is clear also that Socrates is the most prominent speaker in most of the dialogues, leading us to suspect that he is the spokesman for Plato. Nevertheless, Socrates does not always take the leading role. A younger Socrates takes a backseat to Parmenides in the dialogue named after that Italian philosopher. Similarly, the Eleatic stranger takes the lead in the discussions that make up the *Sophist* and the *Statesman*. Socrates does not appear at all in the *Laws*, Plato's massive, unfinished final dialogue. Finally, as noted above, many dialogues in which Socrates takes the lead, including *Euthyphro*, do not come to firm conclusions on the matters under discussion, ending instead in *aporia*.[14] All of these factors and others combine to make the interpretation of a Platonic dialogue a risky operation.

In the face of such interpretive difficulties, what is a reader to do? A partial answer leads us back to the world of performance that constituted the norms of Greek society. If we assume, together with the *Seventh Letter*, that understanding arises from the give-and-take of live conversation, the dialogue's ability to divide the discussion between one or more participants is a way of simulating the dynamic exchange of ideas produced by a live performance. Further, by witnessing this exchange as readers, we are compelled to proceed through all of the intermediate steps of the argument—to consider alternatives and pursue dead ends—rather than skipping to the conclusions; that is, we are compelled to consider the discussed ideas from the perspective of each participant, not just that of Socrates. If this approach is correct, we can surmise that Plato assigned more importance to reader participation in the process of reflection and analysis than to coming to dogmatic conclusions, no matter how well justified.

An anecdote from *Phaedo* illustrates this attitude well. Socrates and the men who visit him in prison are discussing the immortality of the soul from the perspective of reincarnation—specifically, the idea that the soul could be extremely durable and, although able to survive multiple reincarnations, still wear out gradually and, at some point, perish. The group is despondent at this discouraging prospect, until Socrates comforts the men and warns about the dangers of "misology," a chronic distrust of arguments. According to Phaedo, who narrates the entire conversation to a friend, Socrates' intervention "healed our wounds, rallied our scattered forces, and encouraged us to join him in pursuing the inquiry" (89a5–a7). Socrates' warning about misology is not just part of his attempt to prolong the conversation in which he participates. His time is running out anyway; at the end of the dialogue, Socrates drinks the hemlock and dies. The danger of misology, then, is not that it stops Socrates from talking (the Athenian state has already decided to do that on its own) but that serious conversation itself will die. If that happens, Socrates'

14. Other dialogues ending in *aporia* are *Laches*, *Lysis*, *Charmides*, *Theaetetus*, and *Hippias Major*. Platonic dialogues are never easy to catalog precisely, however. Other dialogues contain elements of *aporia* as well.

contemporaries, like many of our own, will simply rehash their unexamined opinions, without listening to objections or listening carefully to opinions different from their own. For Socrates, when this happens, the *logos* indeed dies, and there is not always a Socrates present to tease it back into the realm of the living. All is not lost, however: friends and even solitary individuals can revive the *logos* if they are persistent and focused on examining the best way to live. They also have a precious resource at their disposal: Plato's work itself. In this sense, the Platonic dialogue is a text designed to simulate our encounter with ideas that play an important part in our understanding of our own lives. Following Socrates' warning requires us to continue the war against misology by engaging intellectually with the dialogue and testing our understanding of it in conversation with others, rather than retreating into the echo chamber of habit and received opinion. For this reason, it is more important today than ever that we continue to read Plato's dialogues.

Euthyphro *and the Platonic Corpus*

As far as we know, the Platonic dialogues have come down to us in their entirety. Diogenes Laertius says that they were studied at the Alexandrian library by Aristophanes of Byzantium and others. The arrangement we now have consists of nine tetralogies and is the result of an edition supposedly made in the first century CE by Thrasyllus (D.L. 3.56), traditionally thought to have been astrologer of the emperor Tiberius. The first tetralogy contains the dialogues connected directly with the trial and execution of Socrates: *Euthyphro*, the *Apology, Crito, and Phaedo.* The arrangement of these dialogues follows their dramatic action.[15] *Euthyphro* is the earliest, depicting a conversation in the days leading up to the trial of Socrates. The *Apology* purports to be the speech given by Socrates before the court. *Crito* takes place after the trial. Socrates tells of a dream that he interprets as predicting that his execution is imminent. As has already been noted, *Phaedo* takes place on the final day of Socrates' life and concludes with his death.

The Thrasyllan organization of the dialogues implies nothing about the order in which they were written. Scholars have proposed many different solutions to this problem, but many chronological schemata have been based on questionable criteria, such as the presence of certain philosophic themes like the status of the Forms, a theory assumed to have developed chronologically over Plato's life. Stylistic analysis of the dialogues on the basis of features like

---

15. The first tetralogy does not include the *Theaetetus*, which concludes with Socrates leaving the conversation to attend the meeting with the archon basileus that is the backdrop of *Euthyphro*.

particle combinations (assumed to be largely unconscious) has created a rough consensus, although a full and accurate knowledge of these issues eludes us.[16]

A further reason for a lack of chronological certainty is the relative absence of allusions to contemporary events that could give clues to when Plato wrote the dialogues. This absence is the result of the dialogues' unusual focus on the exploits of Socrates, over and above the circumstances under which Plato himself wrote. The world of the dialogues is the middle to late fifth century, coextensive with the life of Socrates, only a portion of which overlapped with Plato's. Its details, then, are the details that are significant for the fictional world that Plato intends to re-create. The dramatic date of *Parmenides*, for example, is 450 BCE, over two decades earlier than Plato's birth. The occasion of the dialogue, Parmenides' visit to Athens, is an event that has significance only within the world of Socrates. The fictional landscape and the world of the author and his subject sometimes overlap. A few dialogues describe events late in the life of Socrates (see the above discussion of the first tetralogy) and would have seemed contemporary to Plato, but they tell us nothing about the date of the works' composition. Only occasionally, as at the beginning of *Theaetetus* (142a–d), do we find apparent fourth-century anachronisms that could provide at least a *terminus post quem* for the composition of a work. In general, Plato's strong focus on the conversations of Socrates finds few occasions to let in information that does not pertain directly to it.[17] The result are dialogues that have a high degree of verisimilitude but give little indication of the order in which Plato composed them.

It is relevant to ask whether this deficit of information is a tremendous loss for us. If it was correct to say earlier that the intellectual experience of reading a Platonic dialogue is important for creating the right conditions for examining our lives, the order in which we encounter the dialogues may be less important than it would be for a different kind of text.[18] Such a conclusion seems plausible, especially in view of the fact that by structuring his works to occlude their chronological relationships, Plato implies tacitly that his works can be understood adequately without recourse to dating.[19]

---

16. For a recent stylometric analysis of the dialogues, see Ledger 1990.

17. This intense internal focus is not characteristic of all texts. In metatheatrical drama, ancient and modern, appeal to the world of the spectator or of the reader is common. The parabasis of Aristophanic comedy, for example, regularly allows characters to make statements about the author and his views (although they need not be true).

18. Nevertheless, these principles of ordering can have important interpretive consequences. Aristophanes of Byzantium apparently divided the dialogues into trilogies (on analogy with theater?). Neoplatonists later divided them according to their presumed pedagogical use. For a discussion of order and meaning with respect to the dialogues, see Poster 1998.

19. There is also evidence suggesting that Plato revised his works (D.L. 3.37). If reliable, this evidence would pose difficult questions for a chronological approach to the dialogues. Would an early work revised later still be an "early" work?

Background of Euthyphro

Socrates and Euthyphro[20] meet outside the Royal Stoa (*Stoa Basileios*) in the northeast corner of the agora. The building is mentioned by Pausanias and has now been identified by the agora excavators (http://www.agathe.gr/guide/royal_stoa.html). It is called the Royal Stoa because one of its functions was to house the office of the archon basileus, whose duties included the oversight of ancestral sacrifices, cases involving perceived violations of the reverence due to the gods (*graphe asebeias*), the administration of the Eleusinia and other festivals and processions, and private suits for homicide (*hai tou fonou dikai*, *Ath.* 57). Both Socrates and Euthyphro have business with this official, Socrates as the defendant in a *graphe asebeias*, Euthyphro as the prosecutor of a *dike phonou*.

If the procedures used by the archon basileus in cases of alleged *asebeia* were similar to those in place for other types of cases, it is likely that Socrates' meeting involved a process called *anakrisis*, a preliminary meeting with his accuser and the basileus to hear the charges read and to clarify the facts in dispute.[21] The indictment against Socrates would have read something like the version Plato gives in the *Apology*: "Socrates does wrong by not honoring the gods the city honors and bringing in new gods, and he corrupts the youth." Socrates would have denied the validity of the charge. This may have been the first time the litigants met. At any rate, to judge from what he says to Euthyphro, Socrates seems to have little specific knowledge of Meletus beyond his deme and a few physical characteristics. It is therefore possible that at the time at which the *Euthyphro* is set, Socrates has not yet appeared before the basileus. As far as we can tell, he is still on his way to the appointment he mentions at the end of *Theaetetus*.[22]

Piety

The expression *to hosion*, which is the subject of Socrates' questioning of Euthyphro and is loosely translated as "piety," does not exist in our literary sources from the fifth century. The earliest occurrences of the phrase are in the

---

20. For further details about each man, see the commentary herein on *Euthphr.* 1.

21. MacDowell 1978, 239–42. Isaeus 6 suggests that the prosecutor and the defendant could question each other as well. If so, it is hard to see how the reference to "bringing into the city new gods" (*Euthphr.* 3b1–b4) was allowed to stand, given the opinion, expressed at X. *Mem.* 1.1.2–3, that Socrates' belief in the *daimonion* was no stranger than that of people who employed the varied forms of divination practiced by the Greeks.

22. The phrase ὡς ἐγῷμαι at *Euthphr.* 1b9 could refer simply to what Socrates knows by report. It does not show conclusively that he has met Meletus.

Platonic dialogues (most frequently in *Euthyphro*) and Xenophon (*Agesilaus*).[23] When Greeks wanted to talk about religious observance, however, they often used different terms. *Sebeia* often referred to acts of positive devotion such as taking part in public cults and performing traditional sacrifices (*ta patria*). Its opposite, *asebeia*, could refer to the fact that someone neglected these duties; it could also be extended to actions like oath-breaking, which involved the gods as witnesses to the promise.[24] The ephebic oath taken by Athenian boys on the verge of adulthood combined acts of both ritual and promise.[25] By performing these actions, a citizen could reliably imagine that he was fulfilling his traditional obligations to the gods and thus contributing to the short- and long-term prosperity of the city. *Asebeia* is also used more broadly, however, to indicate the range of human behavior thought to bring divine displeasure. This sense of the word figures prominently in the folk tradition. The earliest Greek literature assumes the existence of human beings who come to a bad end because of offenses against the gods. In Book 24 of the *Iliad*, Achilles refers to the case of Niobe, who boasted that her children were much more numerous than those of Leto, whose only children were Artemis and Apollo. Leto retaliated by having Artemis shoot all of Niobe's children, thus cruelly taking away Niobe's sense of superiority (602–09). The notion that all strangers come from Zeus carries with it the idea that the gods sometimes impersonate humans, walk the earth, and punish those who do not shelter guests. *Asebeia* can thus have both a civic dimension and a personal one, two aspects that can also be imagined as overlapping, as in the cases of Oedipus, the tyrant of Thebes who is called on to end a plague by exiling the murderer of Laius (himself) from the city, and Orestes, who is forced to flee Argos after killing his mother to avenge the murder of Agamemnon, his father and the king of Argos.[26]

This overlap can be seen clearly in our dialogue. Euthyphro justifies his

---

23. Comparable expressions occur occasionally in fifth-century texts, such as E. *Helen* 952: ἀλλ᾽ οὐχὶ τοῦτο τὸ καλόν, "This is not nobility." It is possible that their explosion in Plato represents his preservation of an authentic Socratic trait. It is also possible, however, that the usage of such expressions in authors like Euripides suggested to Plato a way of getting beyond the anecdotal ("making this sacrifice is pious," "this man is a good soldier," etc.) to the intellectual idea of nobility, beauty, piety, and goodness. This type of idiom may also have led Plato to the line of analysis that culminates in the Theory of Forms, according to which everything rightly called beautiful is linked to other beautiful things by having a relationship to the "form" of the Beautiful.

24. The range of phenomena that could be included is large, but *asebia* generally referred to actions, not to thoughts or beliefs. For a more complete account, see Dover 1994, 249–50. See also Mikalson 1983, 91–105.

25. For the text of and commentary on the oath, see Rhodes and Osbourne 2003, 441–48.

26. See also Athenaeus 10.437b–e, for the etiology of Choës, the second day of the Anthesteria festival. Confronted by both the need to be hospitable to Orestes and the fear that his pollution would harm them, the Athenians compromised for a day by replacing their practice of communal drinking with the use of individual pitchers.

decision to prosecute his father by saying that to avoid doing so would bring pollution upon the city. As in the examples of Oedipus and Orestes, murder defiles the murderer and makes him both hateful to the gods and a danger to whatever city harbors him. Thus, unlike his family, Euthyphro believes that his actions toward his father are not crazy but a higher form of civic action. Scoffing at Socrates' suggestion that a family connection with the murderer should carry any weight at all, Euthyphro is confident that the gods see the situation as he does (4e–5a).

A similar logic regarding pollution informs the prosecution of Socrates. The decision of Meletus and the others to prosecute him for impiety—on the grounds that he neglected the gods of the city, introduced new ones, and, in so doing, corrupted the youth (cf. *Euthphr.* 3c)—implies that Socrates was in violation of the long-established relationship between the city and the gods that sustained it. Whether justified or not, the charge is a serious one. If Socrates is *asebes*, his presence among the Athenians is potentially so fundamentally noxious to his fellow citizens that—like Oedipus—he cannot even be allowed to remain among them.[27] In this way, the pollution theme that informs *Euthyphro* is not a piece of incidental local color but sets the characters of Socrates and Euthyphro directly within a well-articulated context for examining the relation between the individual, the state, and the often-mysterious workings of the gods.

The Accusers of Socrates

In the *Apology*, Socrates refers to three prosecutors: Meletus, Anytus, and Lycon, who are said to prosecute "on behalf of" the poets, the statesmen and the craftsmen, and the orators, respectively (23e–24a). We do not know exactly what this perplexing statement means or why these groups have a special interest in crimes of *asebeia*. Anytus and Lycon are fairly well known, if the individuals that appear in our sources refer to the accusers of Socrates and not to different Athenians with the same names. According to Socrates (*Euthphr.* 1c), Meletus is less well known, although his father (of the same name) may well have been a writer of tragedies.

---

27. That Socrates participated regularly in public sacrifices is emphasized by Xenophon at *Ap.* 11. See also *Mem.* 1.2. However, if the accusers were correct, Socrates would have added to the pollution by performing these ritual actions in a state of defilement. In fact, a contemporary of Socrates, Andocides, was prosecuted for attending the Eleusinian Mysteries and for depositing a myrtle bough on the altar of Demeter and Persephone in the City Eleusinion, in violation of the decree of Isotimides, which forbade someone who had confessed to *asebeia* from entering the temples of the agora. For Andocides' defense (the speech *On the Mysteries*), with commentary, see MacDowell 1962.

Lycon (*PA* 9271; Nails 2002, 188–89) was sufficiently well known to be mocked in comedy (e.g., Ar. *V.* 1301). He was a significant figure in the democracy during the last decade of the fifth century. He does not appear in the Platonic corpus outside the *Apology*. He is an important character in Xenophon's *Symposium*, however, where he is portrayed as friendly to Socrates, his fellow symposiast. Lycon is also depicted as a devoted father to Autolycus, victor in the boys' pancratium of 422. Autolycus was later executed by the Thirty, a fact that could explain Lycon's personal involvement in the trial of Socrates, if Lycon believed that Socrates was indirectly responsible for Autolycus's death.[28]

Anytus (*PA, APF* 1324; Nails 2002, 37–38) was a prominent figure in late fifth-century Athens. He served as a general in 409 and initially was associated with the Thirty, who later banished him and probably confiscated his property. He joined the exiled democrats in Phyle and was an important figure in the restored democracy. He plays a significant role in Plato's *Meno*, where Anytus becomes angry with Socrates and implies that Socrates' style of questioning will get the philosopher into trouble (94e).

Meletus (*PA* 9825; Nails 2002, 202) is represented as the primary accuser of Socrates, both in *Euthyphro* (2c–3a) and in the *Apology*, where only he is questioned by Socrates (24c–28a). Socrates states clearly that Meletus is not well known, a detail that allows us to rule out several possibilities for his identity. Socrates' claim that Meletus prosecutes "on behalf of the poets" (23c) leads one to believe that he could be the son of the Meletus mocked by Aristophanes (*Ra.* 1303). Diogenes Laertius (2.43) cites the unlikely tradition that Meletus was executed by the Athenians after they repented of the execution of Socrates and that Anytus and Lycon were banished.

---

28. It has sometimes been thought that the friendliness between Lycon and Socrates in Xenophon is inconsistent with the idea of Lycon as a prosecutor of Socrates and that Xenophon and Plato refer to two different people of the same name. This conclusion is possible, but it may well be that putting Socrates and Lycon together in a friendly relationship—and portraying Socrates as attempting to educate Callias on how to show appropriate friendship for his *eromenos* Autolycus (*Smp.* 8.12)—is part of Xenophon's strategy for depicting Socrates as having been wronged by those whom he had directly benefited. See also Plato, *Seventh Letter* 325.

Text

Euthyphro

ΕΥΘ. Τί νεώτερον, ὦ Σώκρατες, γέγονεν, ὅτι σὺ τὰς ἐν   **2a**
Λυκείῳ καταλιπὼν διατριβὰς ἐνθάδε νῦν διατρίβεις περὶ
τὴν τοῦ βασιλέως στοάν; οὐ γάρ που καὶ σοί γε δίκη τις
οὖσα τυγχάνει πρὸς τὸν βασιλέα ὥσπερ ἐμοί.

ΣΩ. Οὔτοι δὴ Ἀθηναῖοί γε, ὦ Εὐθύφρων, δίκην αὐτὴν   5
καλοῦσιν, ἀλλὰ γραφήν.

ΕΥΘ. Τί φής; γραφὴν σέ τις, ὡς ἔοικε, γέγραπται· οὐ   **b**
γὰρ ἐκεῖνό γε καταγνώσομαι, ὡς σὺ ἕτερον.

ΣΩ. Οὐ γὰρ οὖν.

ΕΥΘ. Ἀλλὰ σὲ ἄλλος;

ΣΩ. Πάνυ γε.   5

ΕΥΘ. Τίς οὗτος;

ΣΩ. Οὐδ᾽ αὐτὸς πάνυ τι γιγνώσκω, ὦ Εὐθύφρων, τὸν
ἄνδρα, νέος γάρ τίς μοι φαίνεται καὶ ἀγνώς· ὀνομάζουσι
μέντοι αὐτόν, ὡς ἐγῷμαι, Μέλητον. ἔστι δὲ τῶν δήμων
Πιτθεύς, εἴ τινα νῷ ἔχεις Πιτθέα Μέλητον, οἷον τετανότριχα   10
καὶ οὐ πάνυ εὐγένειον, ἐπίγρυπον δέ.

ΕΥΘ. Οὐκ ἐννοῶ, ὦ Σώκρατες· ἀλλὰ δὴ τίνα γραφὴν
σε γέγραπται;   **c**

ΣΩ. Ἥντινα; οὐκ ἀγεννῆ, ἔμοιγε δοκεῖ· τὸ γὰρ νέον
ὄντα τοσοῦτον πρᾶγμα ἐγνωκέναι οὐ φαῦλόν ἐστιν. ἐκεῖνος

γάρ, ὥς φησιν, οἶδε τίνα τρόπον οἱ νέοι διαφθείρονται καὶ
τίνες οἱ διαφθείροντες αὐτούς. καὶ κινδυνεύει σοφός τις   5
εἶναι, καὶ τὴν ἐμὴν ἀμαθίαν κατιδὼν ὡς διαφθείροντος
τοὺς ἡλικιώτας αὐτοῦ, ἔρχεται κατηγορήσων μου ὥσπερ
πρὸς μητέρα πρὸς τὴν πόλιν. καὶ φαίνεταί μοι τῶν πολιτικῶν
μόνος ἄρχεσθαι ὀρθῶς· ὀρθῶς γάρ ἐστι τῶν νέων   d
πρῶτον ἐπιμεληθῆναι ὅπως ἔσονται ὅτι ἄριστοι, ὥσπερ γεωργὸν
ἀγαθὸν τῶν νέων φυτῶν εἰκὸς πρῶτον ἐπιμεληθῆναι,
μετὰ δὲ τοῦτο καὶ τῶν ἄλλων. καὶ δὴ καὶ
Μέλητος ἴσως πρῶτον μὲν ἡμᾶς ἐκκαθαίρει τοὺς τῶν νέων   3a
τὰς βλάστας διαφθείροντας, ὥς φησιν· ἔπειτα μετὰ τοῦτο
δῆλον ὅτι τῶν πρεσβυτέρων ἐπιμεληθεὶς πλείστων καὶ
μεγίστων ἀγαθῶν αἴτιος τῇ πόλει γενήσεται, ὥς γε τὸ
εἰκὸς συμβῆναι ἐκ τοιαύτης ἀρχῆς ἀρξαμένῳ.   5

ΕΥΘ.   Βουλοίμην ἄν, ὦ Σώκρατες, ἀλλ᾽ ὀρρωδῶ μὴ
τοὐναντίον γένηται· ἀτεχνῶς γάρ μοι δοκεῖ ἀφ᾽ ἑστίας
ἄρχεσθαι κακουργεῖν τὴν πόλιν, ἐπιχειρῶν ἀδικεῖν σέ. καί
μοι λέγε, τί καὶ ποιοῦντά σέ φησι διαφθείρειν τοὺς νέους;

ΣΩ.   Ἄτοπα, ὦ θαυμάσιε, ὡς οὕτω γ᾽ ἀκοῦσαι. φησὶ   b
γάρ με ποιητὴν εἶναι θεῶν, καὶ ὡς καινοὺς ποιοῦντα θεούς,
τοὺς δ᾽ ἀρχαίους οὐ νομίζοντα ἐγράψατο τούτων αὐτῶν
ἕνεκα, ὥς φησιν.

ΕΥΘ.   Μανθάνω, ὦ Σώκρατες· ὅτι δὴ σὺ τὸ δαιμόνιον   5
φὴς σαυτῷ ἑκάστοτε γίγνεσθαι. ὡς οὖν καινοτομοῦντός
σου περὶ τὰ θεῖα γέγραπται ταύτην τὴν γραφήν, καὶ ὡς
διαβαλῶν δὴ ἔρχεται εἰς τὸ δικαστήριον, εἰδὼς ὅτι
εὐδιάβολα τὰ τοιαῦτα πρὸς τοὺς πολλούς. καὶ ἐμοῦ γάρ
τοι, ὅταν τι λέγω ἐν τῇ ἐκκλησίᾳ περὶ τῶν θείων, προλέγων   c
αὐτοῖς τὰ μέλλοντα, καταγελῶσιν ὡς μαινομένου· καίτοι
οὐδὲν ὅτι οὐκ ἀληθὲς εἴρηκα ὧν προεῖπον, ἀλλ᾽ ὅμως
φθονοῦσιν ἡμῖν πᾶσι τοῖς τοιούτοις. ἀλλ᾽ οὐδὲν αὐτῶν χρὴ
φροντίζειν, ἀλλ᾽ ὁμόσε ἰέναι.   5

ΣΩ.   Ὦ φίλε Εὐθύφρων, ἀλλὰ τὸ μὲν καταγελασθῆναι
ἴσως οὐδὲν πρᾶγμα. Ἀθηναίοις γάρ τοι, ὡς ἐμοὶ δοκεῖ, οὐ
σφόδρα μέλει ἄν τινα δεινὸν οἴωνται εἶναι, μὴ μέντοι
διδασκαλικὸν τῆς αὑτοῦ σοφίας· ὃν δ᾽ ἂν καὶ ἄλλους
οἴωνται ποιεῖν τοιούτους, θυμοῦνται, εἴτ᾽ οὖν φθόνῳ ὡς σὺ   d
λέγεις, εἴτε δι᾽ ἄλλο τι.

ΕΥΘ. Τούτου οὖν πέρι ὅπως ποτὲ πρὸς ἐμὲ ἔχουσιν, οὐ
πάνυ ἐπιθυμῶ πειραθῆναι.

ΣΩ. Ἴσως γὰρ σὺ μὲν δοκεῖς σπάνιον σεαυτὸν παρέχειν 5
καὶ διδάσκειν οὐκ ἐθέλειν τὴν σεαυτοῦ σοφίαν· ἐγὼ δὲ
φοβοῦμαι μὴ ὑπὸ φιλανθρωπίας δοκῶ αὐτοῖς ὅτιπερ ἔχω
ἐκκεχυμένως παντὶ ἀνδρὶ λέγειν, οὐ μόνον ἄνευ μισθοῦ,
ἀλλὰ καὶ προστιθεὶς ἂν ἡδέως εἴ τίς μου ἐθέλοι ἀκούειν. εἰ
μὲν οὖν, ὃ νυνδὴ ἔλεγον, μέλλοιέν μου καταγελᾶν, ὥσπερ 10
σὺ φὴς σαυτοῦ, οὐδὲν ἂν εἴη ἀηδὲς παίζοντας καὶ e
γελῶντας ἐν τῷ δικαστηρίῳ διαγαγεῖν· εἰ δὲ σπουδάσονται,
τοῦτ᾽ ἤδη ὅπη ἀποβήσεται ἄδηλον πλὴν ὑμῖν τοῖς μάντεσιν.

ΕΥΘ. Ἀλλ᾽ ἴσως οὐδὲν ἔσται, ὦ Σώκρατες, πρᾶγμα,
ἀλλὰ σύ τε κατὰ νοῦν ἀγωνιῇ τὴν δίκην, οἶμαι δὲ καὶ ἐμὲ 5
τὴν ἐμήν.

ΣΩ. Ἔστιν δὲ δὴ σοί, ὦ Εὐθύφρων, τίς ἡ δίκη; φεύγεις
αὐτὴν ἢ διώκεις;

ΕΥΘ. Διώκω.

ΣΩ. Τίνα; 10

ΕΥΘ. Ὃν διώκων αὖ δοκῶ μαίνεσθαι. **4a**

ΣΩ. Τί δέ; πετόμενόν τινα διώκεις;

ΕΥΘ. Πολλοῦ γε δεῖ πέτεσθαι, ὅς γε τυγχάνει ὢν εὖ
μάλα πρεσβύτης.

ΣΩ. Τίς οὗτος; 5

ΕΥΘ. Ὁ ἐμὸς πατήρ.

ΣΩ. Ὁ σός, ὦ βέλτιστε;

ΕΥΘ. Πάνυ μὲν οὖν.

ΣΩ. Ἔστιν δὲ τί τὸ ἔγκλημα καὶ τίνος ἡ δίκη;

ΕΥΘ.   Φόνου, ὦ Σώκρατες.   10

ΣΩ.   Ἡράκλεις. ἦ που, ὦ Εὐθύφρων, ἀγνοεῖται ὑπὸ
τῶν πολλῶν ὅπη ποτὲ ὀρθῶς ἔχει· οὐ γὰρ οἶμαί γε τοῦ
ἐπιτυχόντος ὀρθῶς αὐτὸ πρᾶξαι, ἀλλὰ πόρρω που ἤδη   **b**
σοφίας ἐλαύνοντος.

ΕΥΘ.   Πόρρω μέντοι νὴ Δία, ὦ Σώκρατες.

ΣΩ.   Ἔστιν δὲ δὴ τῶν οἰκείων τις ὁ τεθνεὼς ὑπὸ τοῦ σοῦ
πατρός; ἢ δῆλα δή; οὐ γὰρ ἄν που ὑπέρ γε ἀλλοτρίου   5
ἐπεξῇσθα φόνου αὐτῷ.

ΕΥΘ.   Γελοῖον, ὦ Σώκρατες, ὅτι οἴει τι διαφέρειν εἴτε
ἀλλότριος εἴτε οἰκεῖος ὁ τεθνεώς, ἀλλ᾽ οὐ τοῦτο μόνον δεῖν
φυλάττειν, εἴτε ἐν δίκῃ ἔκτεινεν ὁ κτείνας εἴτε μή, καὶ εἰ
μὲν ἐν δίκῃ, ἐᾶν, εἰ δὲ μή, ἐπεξιέναι, ἐάνπερ ὁ κτείνας   10
συνέστιός σοι καὶ ὁμοτράπεζος ᾖ· ἴσον γὰρ τὸ μίασμα   **c**
γίγνεται ἐὰν συνῇς τῷ τοιούτῳ συνειδὼς καὶ μὴ ἀφοσιοῖς
σεαυτόν τε καὶ ἐκεῖνον τῇ δίκῃ ἐπεξιών. ἐπεὶ ὅ γε ἀποθανὼν
πελάτης τις ἦν ἐμός, καὶ ὡς ἐγεωργοῦμεν ἐν τῇ
Νάξῳ, ἐθήτευεν ἐκεῖ παρ᾽ ἡμῖν. παροινήσας οὖν καὶ   5
ὀργισθεὶς τῶν οἰκετῶν τινι τῶν ἡμετέρων ἀποσφάττει
αὐτόν. ὁ οὖν πατὴρ συνδήσας τοὺς πόδας καὶ τὰς χεῖρας
αὐτοῦ, καταβαλὼν εἰς τάφρον τινά, πέμπει δεῦρο ἄνδρα
πευσόμενον τοῦ ἐξηγητοῦ ὅτι χρείη ποιεῖν. ἐν δὲ τούτῳ τῷ
χρόνῳ τοῦ δεδεμένου ὠλιγώρει τε καὶ ἠμέλει ὡς ἀνδροφόνου   **d**
καὶ οὐδὲν ὂν πρᾶγμα εἰ καὶ ἀποθάνοι, ὅπερ οὖν καὶ
ἔπαθεν· ὑπὸ γὰρ λιμοῦ καὶ ῥίγους καὶ τῶν δεσμῶν
ἀποθνῄσκει πρὶν τὸν ἄγγελον παρὰ τοῦ ἐξηγητοῦ ἀφικέσθαι.
ταῦτα δὴ οὖν καὶ ἀγανακτεῖ ὅ τε πατὴρ καὶ οἱ ἄλλοι   5
οἰκεῖοι, ὅτι ἐγὼ ὑπὲρ τοῦ ἀνδροφόνου τῷ πατρὶ φόνου ἐπεξέρχομαι,
οὔτε ἀποκτείναντι, ὥς φασιν ἐκεῖνοι, οὔτ᾽ εἰ ὅτι
μάλιστα ἀπέκτεινεν, ἀνδροφόνου γε ὄντος τοῦ ἀποθανόντος,
οὐ δεῖν φροντίζειν ὑπὲρ τοῦ τοιούτου—ἀνόσιον γὰρ
εἶναι τὸ ὑὸν πατρὶ φόνου ἐπεξιέναι—κακῶς εἰδότες, ὦ   **e**
Σώκρατες, τὸ θεῖον ὡς ἔχει τοῦ ὁσίου τε πέρι καὶ τοῦ ἀνοσίου.

ΣΩ.   Σὺ δὲ δὴ πρὸς Διός, ὦ Εὐθύφρων, οὑτωσὶ
ἀκριβῶς οἴει ἐπίστασθαι περὶ τῶν θείων ὅπη ἔχει, καὶ τῶν   5
ὁσίων τε καὶ ἀνοσίων, ὥστε τούτων οὕτω πραχθέντων ὡς

σὺ λέγεις, οὐ φοβῇ δικαζόμενος τῷ πατρὶ ὅπως μὴ αὖ σὺ
ἀνόσιον πρᾶγμα τυγχάνῃς πράττων;

ΕΥΘ. Οὐδὲν γὰρ ἄν μου ὄφελος εἴη, ὦ Σώκρατες,
οὐδέ τῳ ἂν διαφέροι Εὐθύφρων τῶν πολλῶν ἀνθρώπων,   5a
εἰ μὴ τὰ τοιαῦτα πάντα ἀκριβῶς εἰδείην.

ΣΩ. Ἆρ᾽ οὖν μοι, ὦ θαυμάσιε Εὐθύφρων, κράτιστόν
ἐστι μαθητῇ σῷ γενέσθαι, καὶ πρὸ τῆς γραφῆς τῆς πρὸς
Μέλητον αὐτὰ ταῦτα προκαλεῖσθαι αὐτόν, λέγοντα ὅτι   5
ἔγωγε καὶ ἐν τῷ ἔμπροσθεν χρόνῳ τὰ θεῖα περὶ πολλοῦ
ἐποιούμην εἰδέναι, καὶ νῦν, ἐπειδή με ἐκεῖνος αὐτοσχεδιάζοντά
φησι καὶ καινοτομοῦντα περὶ τῶν θείων ἐξαμαρτάνειν,
μαθητὴς δὴ γέγονα σός—"καὶ εἰ μέν, ὦ Μέλητε,"
φαίην ἄν, "Εὐθύφρονα ὁμολογεῖς σοφὸν εἶναι τὰ τοιαῦτα,   b
ὀρθῶς νομίζειν καὶ ἐμὲ ἡγοῦ καὶ μὴ δικάζου· εἰ δὲ μή,
ἐκείνῳ τῷ διδασκάλῳ λάχε δίκην πρότερον ἢ ἐμοί, ὡς
τοὺς πρεσβυτέρους διαφθείροντι, ἐμέ τε καὶ τὸν αὐτοῦ
πατέρα, ἐμὲ μὲν διδάσκοντι, ἐκεῖνον δὲ νουθετοῦντί τε καὶ   5
κολάζοντι"—καὶ ἂν μή μοι πείθηται μηδὲ ἀφίῃ τῆς δίκης
ἢ ἀντ᾽ ἐμοῦ γράφηται σέ, αὐτὰ ταῦτα λέγειν ἐν τῷ
δικαστηρίῳ ἃ προυκαλούμην αὐτόν;

ΕΥΘ. Ναὶ μὰ Δία, ὦ Σώκρατες, εἰ ἄρα ἐμὲ ἐπιχειρήσειε
γράφεσθαι, εὕροιμ᾽ ἄν, ὡς οἶμαι, ὅπῃ σαθρός ἐστιν,   c
καὶ πολὺ ἂν ἡμῖν πρότερον περὶ ἐκείνου λόγος ἐγένετο
ἐν τῷ δικαστηρίῳ ἢ περὶ ἐμοῦ.

ΣΩ. Καὶ ἐγώ τοι, ὦ φίλε ἑταῖρε, ταῦτα γιγνώσκων
μαθητὴς ἐπιθυμῶ γενέσθαι σός, εἰδὼς ὅτι καὶ ἄλλος πού   5
τις καὶ ὁ Μέλητος οὗτος σὲ μὲν οὐδὲ δοκεῖ ὁρᾶν, ἐμὲ δὲ
οὕτως ὀξέως καὶ ῥᾳδίως κατεῖδεν ὥστε ἀσεβείας ἐγράψατο.
νῦν οὖν πρὸς Διὸς λέγε μοι ὃ νυνδὴ σαφῶς εἰδέναι
διισχυρίζου, ποῖόν τι τὸ εὐσεβὲς φῂς εἶναι καὶ τὸ ἀσεβὲς
καὶ περὶ φόνου καὶ περὶ τῶν ἄλλων; ἢ οὐ ταὐτόν ἐστιν ἐν   d
πάσῃ πράξει τὸ ὅσιον αὐτὸ αὑτῷ, καὶ τὸ ἀνόσιον αὖ τοῦ
μὲν ὁσίου παντὸς ἐναντίον, αὐτὸ δὲ αὑτῷ ὅμοιον καὶ ἔχον
μίαν τινὰ ἰδέαν κατὰ τὴν ἀνοσιότητα πᾶν ὅτιπερ ἂν μέλλῃ
ἀνόσιον εἶναι;   5

ΕΥΘ. Πάντως δήπου, ὦ Σώκρατες.

ΣΩ.   Λέγε δή, τί φὴς εἶναι τὸ ὅσιον καὶ τί τὸ ἀνόσιον;

ΕΥΘ.   Λέγω τοίνυν ὅτι τὸ μὲν ὅσιόν ἐστιν ὅπερ ἐγὼ νῦν
ποιῶ, τῷ ἀδικοῦντι ἢ περὶ φόνους ἢ περὶ ἱερῶν κλοπὰς ἤ τι
ἄλλο τῶν τοιούτων ἐξαμαρτάνοντι ἐπεξιέναι, ἐάντε πατὴρ   10
ὢν τυγχάνῃ ἐάντε μήτηρ ἐάντε ἄλλος ὁστισοῦν, τὸ δὲ μὴ   e
ἐπεξιέναι ἀνόσιον· ἐπεί, ὦ Σώκρατες, θέασαι ὡς μέγα σοι
ἐρῶ τεκμήριον τοῦ νόμου ὅτι οὕτως ἔχει—ὃ καὶ ἄλλοις
ἤδη εἶπον, ὅτι ταῦτα ὀρθῶς ἂν εἴη οὕτω γιγνόμενα, μὴ ἐπιτρέπειν
τῷ ἀσεβοῦντι μηδ᾽ ἂν ὁστισοῦν τυγχάνῃ ὤν. αὐτοὶ γὰρ   5
οἱ ἄνθρωποι τυγχάνουσι νομίζοντες τὸν Δία τῶν θεῶν
ἄριστον καὶ δικαιότατον, καὶ τοῦτον ὁμολογοῦσι τὸν αὑτοῦ   6a
πατέρα δῆσαι ὅτι τοὺς ὑεῖς κατέπινεν οὐκ ἐν δίκῃ, κἀκεῖνόν
γε αὖ τὸν αὑτοῦ πατέρα ἐκτεμεῖν δι᾽ ἕτερα τοιαῦτα· ἐμοὶ δὲ
χαλεπαίνουσιν ὅτι τῷ πατρὶ ἐπεξέρχομαι ἀδικοῦντι, καὶ
οὕτως αὐτοὶ αὑτοῖς τὰ ἐναντία λέγουσι περί τε τῶν θεῶν   5
καὶ περὶ ἐμοῦ.

ΣΩ.   Ἆρά γε, ὦ Εὐθύφρων, τοῦτ᾽ ἔστιν οὗ ἕνεκα τὴν
γραφὴν φεύγω, ὅτι τὰ τοιαῦτα ἐπειδάν τις περὶ τῶν θεῶν
λέγῃ, δυσχερῶς πως ἀποδέχομαι; διὸ δή, ὡς ἔοικε, φήσει
τίς με ἐξαμαρτάνειν. νῦν οὖν εἰ καὶ σοὶ ταῦτα συνδοκεῖ τῷ   10
εὖ εἰδότι περὶ τῶν τοιούτων, ἀνάγκη δή, ὡς ἔοικε, καὶ ἡμῖν   b
συγχωρεῖν. τί γὰρ καὶ φήσομεν, οἵ γε καὶ αὐτοὶ ὁμολογοῦμεν
περὶ αὐτῶν μηδὲν εἰδέναι; ἀλλά μοι εἰπὲ πρὸς
Φιλίου, σὺ ὡς ἀληθῶς ἡγῇ ταῦτα οὕτως γεγονέναι;

ΕΥΘ.   Καὶ ἔτι γε τούτων θαυμασιώτερα, ὦ Σώκρατες,   5
ἃ οἱ πολλοὶ οὐκ ἴσασιν.

ΣΩ.   Καὶ πόλεμον ἄρα ἡγῇ σὺ εἶναι τῷ ὄντι ἐν τοῖς θεοῖς
πρὸς ἀλλήλους, καὶ ἔχθρας γε δεινὰς καὶ μάχας καὶ ἄλλα
τοιαῦτα πολλά, οἷα λέγεταί τε ὑπὸ τῶν ποιητῶν, καὶ ὑπὸ
τῶν ἀγαθῶν γραφέων τά τε ἄλλα ἱερὰ ἡμῖν καταπεποίκιλται,   c
καὶ δὴ καὶ τοῖς μεγάλοις Παναθηναίοις ὁ πέπλος
μεστὸς τῶν τοιούτων ποικιλμάτων ἀνάγεται εἰς τὴν ἀκρόπολιν;
ταῦτα ἀληθῆ φῶμεν εἶναι, ὦ Εὐθύφρων;

ΕΥΘ.   Μὴ μόνον γε, ὦ Σώκρατες, ἀλλ᾽ ὅπερ ἄρτι εἶπον,   5
καὶ ἄλλα σοι ἐγὼ πολλά, ἐάνπερ βούλῃ, περὶ τῶν θείων
διηγήσομαι, ἃ σὺ ἀκούων εὖ οἶδ᾽ ὅτι ἐκπλαγήσῃ.

ΣΩ. Οὐκ ἂν θαυμάζοιμι. ἀλλὰ ταῦτα μέν μοι εἰς αὖθις
ἐπὶ σχολῆς διηγήσῃ· νυνὶ δὲ ὅπερ ἄρτι σε ἠρόμην πειρῶ
σαφέστερον εἰπεῖν. οὐ γάρ με, ὦ ἑταῖρε, τὸ πρότερον   d
ἱκανῶς ἐδίδαξας ἐρωτήσαντα τὸ ὅσιον ὅτι ποτ᾽ εἴη, ἀλλά
μοι εἶπες ὅτι τοῦτο τυγχάνει ὅσιον ὂν ὃ σὺ νῦν ποιεῖς,
φόνου ἐπεξιὼν τῷ πατρί.

ΕΥΘ. Καὶ ἀληθῆ γε ἔλεγον, ὦ Σώκρατες.   5

ΣΩ. Ἴσως. ἀλλὰ γάρ, ὦ Εὐθύφρων, καὶ ἄλλα πολλὰ
φῂς εἶναι ὅσια.

ΕΥΘ. Καὶ γὰρ ἔστιν.

ΣΩ. Μέμνησαι οὖν ὅτι οὐ τοῦτό σοι διεκελευόμην, ἕν τι
ἢ δύο με διδάξαι τῶν πολλῶν ὁσίων, ἀλλ᾽ ἐκεῖνο αὐτὸ τὸ   10
εἶδος ᾧ πάντα τὰ ὅσια ὅσιά ἐστιν; ἔφησθα γάρ που μιᾷ
ἰδέᾳ τά τε ἀνόσια ἀνόσια εἶναι καὶ τὰ ὅσια ὅσια· ἢ οὐ   e
μνημονεύεις;

ΕΥΘ. Ἔγωγε.

ΣΩ. Ταύτην τοίνυν με αὐτὴν δίδαξον τὴν ἰδέαν τίς ποτέ
ἐστιν, ἵνα εἰς ἐκείνην ἀποβλέπων καὶ χρώμενος αὐτῇ   5
παραδείγματι, ὃ μὲν ἂν τοιοῦτον ᾖ ὧν ἂν ἢ σὺ ἢ ἄλλος τις
πράττῃ φῶ ὅσιον εἶναι, ὃ δ᾽ ἂν μὴ τοιοῦτον, μὴ φῶ.

ΕΥΘ. Ἀλλ᾽ εἰ οὕτω βούλει, ὦ Σώκρατες, καὶ οὕτω σοι φράσω.

ΣΩ. Ἀλλὰ μὴν βούλομαί γε.

ΕΥΘ. Ἔστι τοίνυν τὸ μὲν τοῖς θεοῖς προσφιλὲς ὅσιον,   10
τὸ δὲ μὴ προσφιλὲς ἀνόσιον.   **7a**

ΣΩ. Παγκάλως, ὦ Εὐθύφρων, καὶ ὡς ἐγὼ ἐζήτουν
ἀποκρίνασθαί σε, οὕτω νῦν ἀπεκρίνω. εἰ μέντοι ἀληθῶς,
τοῦτο οὔπω οἶδα, ἀλλὰ σὺ δῆλον ὅτι ἐπεκδιδάξεις ὡς ἔστιν
ἀληθῆ ἃ λέγεις.   5

ΕΥΘ. Πάνυ μὲν οὖν.

ΣΩ.   Φέρε δή, ἐπισκεψώμεθα τί λέγομεν. τὸ μὲν
θεοφιλές τε καὶ θεοφιλὴς ἄνθρωπος ὅσιος, τὸ δὲ θεομισὲς
καὶ ὁ θεομισὴς ἀνόσιος· οὐ ταὐτὸν δ' ἐστίν, ἀλλὰ τὸ
ἐναντιώτατον, τὸ ὅσιον τῷ ἀνοσίῳ· οὐχ οὕτως;   10

ΕΥΘ.   Οὕτω μὲν οὖν.

ΣΩ.   Καὶ εὖ γε φαίνεται εἰρῆσθαι;

ΕΥΘ.   Δοκῶ, ὦ Σώκρατες.   **b**

ΣΩ.   Οὐκοῦν καὶ ὅτι στασιάζουσιν οἱ θεοί,
ὦ Εὐθύφρων, καὶ διαφέρονται ἀλλήλοις καὶ ἔχθρα ἐστὶν ἐν
αὐτοῖς πρὸς ἀλλήλους, καὶ τοῦτο εἴρηται;

ΕΥΘ.   Εἴρηται γάρ.   5

ΣΩ.   Ἔχθραν δὲ καὶ ὀργάς, ὦ ἄριστε, ἡ περὶ τίνων διαφορὰ
ποιεῖ; ὧδε δὲ σκοπῶμεν. ἆρ' ἂν εἰ διαφεροίμεθα ἐγώ
τε καὶ σὺ περὶ ἀριθμοῦ ὁπότερα πλείω, ἡ περὶ τούτων διαφορὰ
ἐχθροὺς ἂν ἡμᾶς ποιοῖ καὶ ὀργίζεσθαι ἀλλήλοις, ἢ
ἐπὶ λογισμὸν ἐλθόντες περί γε τῶν τοιούτων ταχὺ ἂν   10
ἀπαλλαγεῖμεν;   **c**

ΕΥΘ.   Πάνυ γε.

ΣΩ.   Οὐκοῦν καὶ περὶ τοῦ μείζονος καὶ ἐλάττονος εἰ
διαφεροίμεθα, ἐπὶ τὸ μετρεῖν ἐλθόντες ταχὺ παυσαίμεθ' ἂν
τῆς διαφορᾶς;   5

ΕΥΘ.   Ἔστι ταῦτα.

ΣΩ.   Καὶ ἐπί γε τὸ ἱστάναι ἐλθόντες, ὡς ἐγῷμαι, περὶ
τοῦ βαρυτέρου τε καὶ κουφοτέρου διακριθεῖμεν ἄν;

ΕΥΘ.   Πῶς γὰρ οὔ;

ΣΩ.   Περὶ τίνος δὲ δὴ διενεχθέντες καὶ ἐπὶ τίνα κρίσιν   10
οὐ δυνάμενοι ἀφικέσθαι ἐχθροί γε ἂν ἀλλήλοις εἶμεν καὶ
ὀργιζοίμεθα; ἴσως οὐ πρόχειρόν σοί ἐστιν, ἀλλ' ἐμοῦ
λέγοντος σκόπει εἰ τάδε ἐστὶ τό τε δίκαιον καὶ τὸ ἄδικον   **d**
καὶ καλὸν καὶ αἰσχρὸν καὶ ἀγαθὸν καὶ κακόν. ἆρα οὐ

ταῦτά ἐστιν περὶ ὧν διενεχθέντες καὶ οὐ δυνάμενοι ἐπὶ
ἱκανὴν κρίσιν αὐτῶν ἐλθεῖν ἐχθροὶ ἀλλήλοις γιγνόμεθα,
ὅταν γιγνώμεθα, καὶ ἐγὼ καὶ σὺ καὶ οἱ ἄλλοι ἄνθρωποι   5
πάντες;

ΕΥΘ. Ἀλλ᾽ ἔστιν αὕτη ἡ διαφορά, ὦ Σώκρατες, καὶ
περὶ τούτων.

ΣΩ. Τί δὲ οἱ θεοί, ὦ Εὐθύφρων; οὐκ εἴπερ τι διαφέρονται, δι᾽ αὐτὰ ταῦτα διαφέροιντ᾽ ἄν;   10

ΕΥΘ. Πολλὴ ἀνάγκη.

ΣΩ. Καὶ τῶν θεῶν ἄρα, ὦ γενναῖε Εὐθύφρων, ἄλλοι   e
ἄλλα δίκαια ἡγοῦνται κατὰ τὸν σὸν λόγον, καὶ καλὰ καὶ
αἰσχρὰ καὶ ἀγαθὰ καὶ κακά· οὐ γὰρ ἄν που ἐστασίαζον
ἀλλήλοις εἰ μὴ περὶ τούτων διεφέροντο· ἢ γάρ;

ΕΥΘ. Ὀρθῶς λέγεις.   5

ΣΩ. Οὐκοῦν ἅπερ καλὰ ἡγοῦνται ἕκαστοι καὶ ἀγαθὰ
καὶ δίκαια, ταῦτα καὶ φιλοῦσιν, τὰ δὲ ἐναντία τούτων
μισοῦσιν;

ΕΥΘ. Πάνυ γε.

ΣΩ. Ταὐτὰ δέ γε, ὡς σὺ φής, οἱ μὲν δίκαια ἡγοῦνται,   10
οἱ δὲ ἄδικα, περὶ ἃ καὶ ἀμφισβητοῦντες στασιάζουσί τε καὶ **8a**
πολεμοῦσιν ἀλλήλοις· ἆρα οὐχ οὕτω;

ΕΥΘ. Οὕτω.

ΣΩ. Ταῦτ᾽ ἄρα, ὡς ἔοικεν, μισεῖταί τε ὑπὸ τῶν θεῶν καὶ
φιλεῖται, καὶ θεομισῆ τε καὶ θεοφιλῆ ταῦτ᾽ ἂν εἴη.   5

ΕΥΘ. Ἔοικεν.

ΣΩ. Καὶ ὅσια ἄρα καὶ ἀνόσια τὰ αὐτὰ ἂν εἴη, ὦ
Εὐθύφρων, τούτῳ τῷ λόγῳ.

ΕΥΘ. Κινδυνεύει.

ΣΩ.   Οὐκ ἄρα ὃ ἠρόμην ἀπεκρίνω, ὦ θαυμάσιε. οὐ γὰρ   10
τοῦτό γε ἠρώτων, ὃ τυγχάνει ταὐτὸν ὂν ὅσιόν τε καὶ
ἀνόσιον· ὃ δ᾽ ἂν θεοφιλὲς ᾖ καὶ θεομισές ἐστιν, ὡς ἔοικεν.
ὥστε, ὦ Εὐθύφρων, ὃ σὺ νῦν ποιεῖς τὸν πατέρα κολάζων,   **b**
οὐδὲν θαυμαστὸν εἰ τοῦτο δρῶν τῷ μὲν Διὶ προσφιλὲς
ποιεῖς, τῷ δὲ Κρόνῳ καὶ τῷ Οὐρανῷ ἐχθρόν, καὶ τῷ μὲν
Ἡφαίστῳ φίλον, τῇ δὲ Ἥρᾳ ἐχθρόν, καὶ εἴ τις ἄλλος τῶν
θεῶν ἕτερος ἑτέρῳ διαφέρεται περὶ αὐτοῦ, καὶ ἐκείνοις   5
κατὰ τὰ αὐτά.

ΕΥΘ.   Ἀλλ᾽ οἶμαι, ὦ Σώκρατες, περί γε τούτου τῶν
θεῶν οὐδένα ἕτερον ἑτέρῳ διαφέρεσθαι, ὡς οὐ δεῖ δίκην
διδόναι ἐκεῖνον ὃς ἂν ἀδίκως τινὰ ἀποκτείνῃ.

ΣΩ.   Τί δέ; ἀνθρώπων, ὦ Εὐθύφρων, ἤδη τινὸς   10
ἤκουσας ἀμφισβητοῦντος ὡς τὸν ἀδίκως ἀποκτείναντα ἢ   **c**
ἄλλο ἀδίκως ποιοῦντα ὁτιοῦν οὐ δεῖ δίκην διδόναι;

ΕΥΘ.   Οὐδὲν μὲν οὖν παύονται ταῦτα ἀμφισβητοῦντες
καὶ ἄλλοθι καὶ ἐν τοῖς δικαστηρίοις· ἀδικοῦντες γὰρ
πάμπολλα, πάντα ποιοῦσι καὶ λέγουσι φεύγοντες τὴν   5
δίκην.

ΣΩ.   Ἦ καὶ ὁμολογοῦσιν, ὦ Εὐθύφρων, ἀδικεῖν, καὶ
ὁμολογοῦντες ὅμως οὐ δεῖν φασὶ σφᾶς διδόναι δίκην;

ΕΥΘ.   Οὐδαμῶς τοῦτό γε.

ΣΩ.   Οὐκ ἄρα πᾶν γε ποιοῦσι καὶ λέγουσι· τοῦτο γὰρ   10
οἶμαι οὐ τολμῶσι λέγειν οὐδ᾽ ἀμφισβητεῖν, ὡς οὐχὶ εἴπερ
ἀδικοῦσί γε δοτέον δίκην, ἀλλ᾽ οἶμαι οὔ φασιν ἀδικεῖν· ἦ   **d**
γάρ;

ΕΥΘ.   Ἀληθῆ λέγεις.

ΣΩ.   Οὐκ ἄρα ἐκεῖνό γε ἀμφισβητοῦσιν, ὡς οὐ τὸν
ἀδικοῦντα δεῖ διδόναι δίκην, ἀλλ᾽ ἐκεῖνο ἴσως ἀμφισβητοῦσιν,   5
τὸ τίς ἐστιν ὁ ἀδικῶν καὶ τί δρῶν καὶ πότε.

ΕΥΘ.   Ἀληθῆ λέγεις.

ΣΩ. Οὐκοῦν αὐτά γε ταῦτα καὶ οἱ θεοὶ πεπόνθασιν,
εἴπερ στασιάζουσι περὶ τῶν δικαίων καὶ ἀδίκων ὡς ὁ σὸς
λόγος, καὶ οἱ μέν φασιν ἀλλήλους ἀδικεῖν, οἱ δὲ οὔ φασιν;   10
ἐπεὶ ἐκεῖνό γε δήπου, ὦ θαυμάσιε, οὐδεὶς οὔτε θεῶν οὔτε
ἀνθρώπων τολμᾷ λέγειν, ὡς οὐ τῷ γε ἀδικοῦντι δοτέον   e
δίκην.

ΕΥΘ. Ναί, τοῦτο μὲν ἀληθὲς λέγεις, ὦ Σώκρατες, τό
γε κεφάλαιον.

ΣΩ. Ἀλλ᾽ ἕκαστόν γε οἶμαι, ὦ Εὐθύφρων, τῶν πραχθέντων   5
ἀμφισβητοῦσιν οἱ ἀμφισβητοῦντες, καὶ ἄνθρωποι
καὶ θεοί, εἴπερ ἀμφισβητοῦσιν θεοί· πράξεώς τινος πέρι
διαφερόμενοι οἱ μὲν δικαίως φασὶν αὐτὴν πεπρᾶχθαι, οἱ δὲ
ἀδίκως· ἆρ᾽ οὐχ οὕτω;

ΕΥΘ. Πάνυ γε.   10

ΣΩ. Ἴθι νυν, ὦ φίλε Εὐθύφρων, δίδαξον καὶ ἐμέ, ἵνα   9a
σοφώτερος γένωμαι, τί σοι τεκμήριόν ἐστιν ὡς πάντες θεοὶ
ἡγοῦνται ἐκεῖνον ἀδίκως τεθνάναι, ὃς ἂν θητεύων ἀνδροφόνος
γενόμενος, συνδεθεὶς ὑπὸ τοῦ δεσπότου τοῦ ἀποθανόντος,
φθάσῃ τελευτήσας διὰ τὰ δεσμὰ πρὶν τὸν   5
συνδήσαντα παρὰ τῶν ἐξηγητῶν περὶ αὐτοῦ πυθέσθαι τί
χρὴ ποιεῖν, καὶ ὑπὲρ τοῦ τοιούτου δὴ ὀρθῶς ἔχει ἐπεξιέναι
καὶ ἐπισκήπτεσθαι φόνου τὸν ὑὸν τῷ πατρί; ἴθι, περὶ
τούτων πειρῶ τί μοι σαφὲς ἐνδείξασθαι ὡς παντὸς μᾶλλον   b
πάντες θεοὶ ἡγοῦνται ὀρθῶς ἔχειν ταύτην τὴν πρᾶξιν· κἂν
μοι ἱκανῶς ἐνδείξῃ, ἐγκωμιάζων σε ἐπὶ σοφίᾳ οὐδέποτε
παύσομαι.

ΕΥΘ. Ἀλλ᾽ ἴσως οὐκ ὀλίγον ἔργον ἐστίν, ὦ Σώκρατες,   5
ἐπεὶ πάνυ γε σαφῶς ἔχοιμι ἂν ἐπιδεῖξαί σοι.

ΣΩ. Μανθάνω· ὅτι σοι δοκῶ τῶν δικαστῶν δυσμαθέστερος
εἶναι, ἐπεὶ ἐκείνοις γε ἐνδείξῃ δῆλον ὅτι ὡς ἄδικά
τέ ἐστιν καὶ οἱ θεοὶ ἅπαντες τὰ τοιαῦτα μισοῦσιν.

ΕΥΘ. Πάνυ γε σαφῶς, ὦ Σώκρατες, ἐάνπερ ἀκούωσί   10
γέ μου λέγοντος.

ΣΩ.   Ἀλλ’ ἀκούσονται, ἐάνπερ εὖ δοκῇς λέγειν. τόδε δέ   c
σου ἐνενόησα ἅμα λέγοντος καὶ πρὸς ἐμαυτὸν σκοπῶ· “εἰ
ὅτι μάλιστά με Εὐθύφρων διδάξειεν ὡς οἱ θεοὶ ἅπαντες τὸν
τοιοῦτον θάνατον ἡγοῦνται ἄδικον εἶναι, τί μᾶλλον ἐγὼ
μεμάθηκα παρ’ Εὐθύφρονος τί ποτ’ ἐστὶν τὸ ὅσιόν τε καὶ τὸ   5
ἀνόσιον; θεομισὲς μὲν γὰρ τοῦτο τὸ ἔργον, ὡς ἔοικεν, εἴη
ἄν. ἀλλὰ γὰρ οὐ τούτῳ ἐφάνη ἄρτι ὡρισμένα τὸ ὅσιον καὶ μή·
τὸ γὰρ θεομισὲς ὂν καὶ θεοφιλὲς ἐφάνη.” ὥστε τούτου
μὲν ἀφίημί σε, ὦ Εὐθύφρων· εἰ βούλει, πάντες αὐτὸ
ἡγείσθων θεοὶ ἄδικον καὶ πάντες μισούντων. ἀλλ’ ἄρα   d
τοῦτο ὃ νῦν ἐπανορθούμεθα ἐν τῷ λόγῳ, ὡς ὃ μὲν ἂν
πάντες οἱ θεοὶ μισῶσιν ἀνόσιόν ἐστιν, ὃ δ’ ἂν φιλῶσιν,
ὅσιον· ὃ δ’ ἂν οἱ μὲν φιλῶσιν οἱ δὲ μισῶσιν, οὐδέτερα ἢ
ἀμφότερα—ἆρ’ οὕτω βούλει ἡμῖν ὡρίσθαι νῦν περὶ τοῦ   5
ὁσίου καὶ τοῦ ἀνοσίου;

ΕΥΘ.   Τί γὰρ κωλύει, ὦ Σώκρατες;

ΣΩ.   Οὐδὲν ἐμέ γε, ὦ Εὐθύφρων, ἀλλὰ σὺ δὴ τὸ σὸν
σκόπει, εἰ τοῦτο ὑποθέμενος οὕτω ῥᾷστά με διδάξεις ὃ
ὑπέσχου.   10

ΕΥΘ.   Ἀλλ’ ἔγωγε φαίην ἂν τοῦτο εἶναι τὸ ὅσιον ὃ ἂν   e
πάντες οἱ θεοὶ φιλῶσιν, καὶ τὸ ἐναντίον, ὃ ἂν πάντες θεοὶ
μισῶσιν, ἀνόσιον.

ΣΩ.   Οὐκοῦν ἐπισκοπῶμεν αὖ τοῦτο, ὦ Εὐθύφρων, εἰ
καλῶς λέγεται, ἢ ἐῶμεν καὶ οὕτω ἡμῶν τε αὐτῶν ἀποδεχώμεθα   5
καὶ τῶν ἄλλων, ἐὰν μόνον φῇ τίς τι ἔχειν οὕτω
συγχωροῦντες ἔχειν; ἢ σκεπτέον τί λέγει ὁ λέγων;

ΕΥΘ.   Σκεπτέον· οἶμαι μέντοι ἔγωγε τοῦτο νυνὶ καλῶς λέγεσθαι.

ΣΩ.   Τάχ’, ὠγαθέ, βέλτιον εἰσόμεθα. ἐννόησον γὰρ τὸ   10a
τοιόνδε· ἆρα τὸ ὅσιον ὅτι ὅσιόν ἐστιν φιλεῖται ὑπὸ τῶν
θεῶν, ἢ ὅτι φιλεῖται ὅσιόν ἐστιν;

ΕΥΘ.   Οὐκ οἶδ’ ὅτι λέγεις, ὦ Σώκρατες.

ΣΩ.   Ἀλλ’ ἐγὼ πειράσομαι σαφέστερον φράσαι. λέγομέν   5
τι φερόμενον καὶ φέρον καὶ ἀγόμενον καὶ ἄγον καὶ

ὁρώμενον καὶ ὁρῶν, καὶ πάντα τὰ τοιαῦτα μανθάνεις ὅτι
ἕτερα ἀλλήλων ἐστὶ καὶ ᾗ ἕτερα;

ΕΥΘ. Ἔγωγέ μοι δοκῶ μανθάνειν.

ΣΩ. Οὐκοῦν καὶ φιλούμενόν τί ἐστιν καὶ τούτου ἕτερον τὸ φιλοῦν;   10

ΕΥΘ. Πῶς γὰρ οὔ;

ΣΩ. Λέγε δή μοι, πότερον τὸ φερόμενον διότι φέρεται   b
φερόμενόν ἐστιν, ἢ δι᾽ ἄλλο τι;

ΕΥΘ. Οὔκ, ἀλλὰ διὰ τοῦτο.

ΣΩ. Καὶ τὸ ἀγόμενον δὴ διότι ἄγεται, καὶ τὸ ὁρώμενον
διότι ὁρᾶται;   5

ΕΥΘ. Πάνυ γε.

ΣΩ. Οὐκ ἄρα διότι ὁρώμενόν γέ ἐστιν, διὰ τοῦτο
ὁρᾶται, ἀλλὰ τὸ ἐναντίον διότι ὁρᾶται, διὰ τοῦτο
ὁρώμενον· οὐδὲ διότι ἀγόμενόν ἐστιν, διὰ τοῦτο ἄγεται,
ἀλλὰ διότι ἄγεται, διὰ τοῦτο ἀγόμενον· οὐδὲ διότι φερόμενον,   10
φέρεται, ἀλλὰ διότι φέρεται, φερόμενον. ἆρα
κατάδηλον, ὦ Εὐθύφρων, ὃ βούλομαι λέγειν; βούλομαι δὲ   c
τόδε, ὅτι εἴ τι γίγνεται ἤ τι πάσχει, οὐχ ὅτι γιγνόμενόν
ἐστι, γίγνεται, ἀλλ᾽ ὅτι γίγνεται, γιγνόμενόν ἐστιν· οὐδ᾽ ὅτι
πάσχον ἐστί, πάσχει, ἀλλ᾽ ὅτι πάσχει, πάσχον ἐστίν· ἢ οὐ
συγχωρεῖς οὕτω;   5

ΕΥΘ. Ἔγωγε.

ΣΩ. Οὐκοῦν καὶ τὸ φιλούμενον ἢ γιγνόμενόν τί ἐστιν ἢ
πάσχον τι ὑπό του;

ΕΥΘ. Πάνυ γε.

ΣΩ. Καὶ τοῦτο ἄρα οὕτως ἔχει ὥσπερ τὰ πρότερα· οὐχ   10
ὅτι φιλούμενόν ἐστιν, φιλεῖται ὑπὸ ὧν φιλεῖται, ἀλλ᾽ ὅτι
φιλεῖται, φιλούμενον;

ΕΥΘ.   Ἀνάγκη.

ΣΩ.   Τί δὴ οὖν λέγομεν περὶ τοῦ ὁσίου, ὦ Εὐθύφρων;   **d**
ἄλλο τι φιλεῖται ὑπὸ θεῶν πάντων, ὡς ὁ σὸς λόγος;

ΕΥΘ.   Ναί.

ΣΩ.   Ἆρα διὰ τοῦτο, ὅτι ὅσιόν ἐστιν, ἢ δι᾽ ἄλλο τι;

ΕΥΘ.   Οὔκ, ἀλλὰ διὰ τοῦτο.   5

ΣΩ.   Διότι ἄρα ὅσιόν ἐστιν, φιλεῖται, ἀλλ᾽ οὐχ ὅτι
φιλεῖται, διὰ τοῦτο ὅσιόν ἐστιν;

ΕΥΘ.   Ἔοικεν.

ΣΩ.   Ἀλλὰ μὲν δὴ διότι γε φιλεῖται ὑπὸ θεῶν, φιλούμενόν
ἐστι καὶ θεοφιλές.   10

ΕΥΘ.   Πῶς γὰρ οὔ;

ΣΩ.   Οὐκ ἄρα τὸ θεοφιλὲς ὅσιόν ἐστιν, ὦ Εὐθύφρων,
οὐδὲ τὸ ὅσιον θεοφιλές, ὡς σὺ λέγεις, ἀλλ᾽ ἕτερον τοῦτο
τούτου.

ΕΥΘ.   Πῶς δή, ὦ Σώκρατες;   **e**

ΣΩ.   Ὅτι ὁμολογοῦμεν τὸ μὲν ὅσιον διὰ τοῦτο φιλεῖσθαι,
ὅτι ὅσιόν ἐστιν, ἀλλ᾽ οὐ διότι φιλεῖται ὅσιον εἶναι· ἢ
γάρ;

ΕΥΘ.   Ναί.   5

ΣΩ.   Τὸ δέ γε θεοφιλὲς ὅτι φιλεῖται ὑπὸ θεῶν, αὐτῷ
τούτῳ τῷ φιλεῖσθαι θεοφιλὲς εἶναι, ἀλλ᾽ οὐχ ὅτι θεοφιλές,
διὰ τοῦτο φιλεῖσθαι.

ΕΥΘ.   Ἀληθῆ λέγεις.

ΣΩ.   Ἀλλ᾽ εἴ γε ταὐτὸν ἦν, ὦ φίλε Εὐθύφρων, τὸ   10
θεοφιλὲς καὶ τὸ ὅσιον, εἰ μὲν διὰ τὸ ὅσιον εἶναι ἐφιλεῖτο τὸ

ὅσιον, καὶ διὰ τὸ θεοφιλὲς εἶναι ἐφιλεῖτο ἂν τὸ θεοφιλές, εἰ   **11a**
δὲ διὰ τὸ φιλεῖσθαι ὑπὸ θεῶν τὸ θεοφιλὲς θεοφιλὲς ἦν, καὶ
τὸ ὅσιον ἂν διὰ τὸ φιλεῖσθαι ὅσιον ἦν· νῦν δὲ ὁρᾷς ὅτι
ἐναντίως ἔχετον, ὡς παντάπασιν ἑτέρω ὄντε ἀλλήλων. τὸ
μὲν γάρ, ὅτι φιλεῖται, ἐστὶν οἷον φιλεῖσθαι· τὸ δ᾽ ὅτι ἐστὶν   5
οἷον φιλεῖσθαι, διὰ τοῦτο φιλεῖται. καὶ κινδυνεύεις, ὦ
Εὐθύφρων, ἐρωτώμενος τὸ ὅσιον ὅτι ποτ᾽ ἐστίν, τὴν μὲν
οὐσίαν μοι αὐτοῦ οὐ βούλεσθαι δηλῶσαι, πάθος δέ τι περὶ
αὐτοῦ λέγειν, ὅτι πέπονθε τοῦτο τὸ ὅσιον, φιλεῖσθαι ὑπὸ
πάντων θεῶν· ὅτι δὲ ὄν, οὔπω εἶπες. εἰ οὖν σοι φίλον, μή με   **b**
ἀποκρύψῃ, ἀλλὰ πάλιν εἰπὲ ἐξ ἀρχῆς τί ποτε ὂν τὸ ὅσιον
εἴτε φιλεῖται ὑπὸ θεῶν εἴτε ὁτιδὴ πάσχει—οὐ γὰρ περὶ
τούτου διοισόμεθα—ἀλλ᾽ εἰπὲ προθύμως τί ἐστιν τό τε
ὅσιον καὶ τὸ ἀνόσιον;   5

ΕΥΘ. Ἀλλ᾽, ὦ Σώκρατες, οὐκ ἔχω ἔγωγε ὅπως σοι
εἴπω ὃ νοῶ· περιέρχεται γάρ πως ἡμῖν ἀεὶ ὃ ἂν προθώμεθα
καὶ οὐκ ἐθέλει μένειν ὅπου ἂν ἱδρυσώμεθα αὐτό.

ΣΩ. Τοῦ ἡμετέρου προγόνου, ὦ Εὐθύφρων, ἔοικεν
εἶναι Δαιδάλου τὰ ὑπὸ σοῦ λεγόμενα. καὶ εἰ μὲν αὐτὰ ἐγὼ   **c**
ἔλεγον καὶ ἐτιθέμην, ἴσως ἄν με ἐπέσκωπτες ὡς ἄρα καὶ
ἐμοὶ κατὰ τὴν ἐκείνου συγγένειαν τὰ ἐν τοῖς λόγοις ἔργα
ἀποδιδράσκει καὶ οὐκ ἐθέλει μένειν ὅπου ἄν τις αὐτὰ θῇ·
νῦν δὲ σαὶ γὰρ αἱ ὑποθέσεις εἰσίν. ἄλλου δή τινος δεῖ   5
σκώμματος· οὐ γὰρ ἐθέλουσι σοὶ μένειν, ὡς καὶ αὐτῷ σοι
δοκεῖ.

ΕΥΘ. Ἐμοὶ δὲ δοκεῖ σχεδόν τι τοῦ αὐτοῦ σκώμματος,
ὦ Σώκρατες, δεῖσθαι τὰ λεγόμενα· τὸ γὰρ περιιέναι αὐτοῖς
τοῦτο καὶ μὴ μένειν ἐν τῷ αὐτῷ οὐκ ἐγώ εἰμι ὁ ἐντιθείς,   10
ἀλλὰ σύ μοι δοκεῖς ὁ Δαίδαλος, ἐπεὶ ἐμοῦ γε ἕνεκα ἔμενεν   **d**
ἂν ταῦτα οὕτως.

ΣΩ. Κινδυνεύω ἄρα, ὦ ἑταῖρε, ἐκείνου τοῦ ἀνδρὸς
δεινότερος γεγονέναι τὴν τέχνην τοσούτῳ, ὅσῳ ὁ μὲν τὰ
αὑτοῦ μόνα ἐποίει οὐ μένοντα, ἐγὼ δὲ πρὸς τοῖς ἐμαυτοῦ,   5
ὡς ἔοικε, καὶ τὰ ἀλλότρια. καὶ δῆτα τοῦτό μοι τῆς τέχνης
ἐστὶ κομψότατον, ὅτι ἄκων εἰμὶ σοφός· ἐβουλόμην γὰρ ἂν
μοι τοὺς λόγους μένειν καὶ ἀκινήτως ἱδρῦσθαι μᾶλλον ἢ
πρὸς τῇ Δαιδάλου σοφίᾳ τὰ Ταντάλου χρήματα γενέσθαι.   **e**

καὶ τούτων μὲν ἄδην· ἐπειδὴ δέ μοι δοκεῖς σὺ τρυφᾶν,
αὐτός σοι συμπροθυμήσομαι ὅπως ἄν με διδάξῃς περὶ τοῦ
ὁσίου. καὶ μὴ προαποκάμῃς· ἰδὲ γὰρ εἰ οὐκ ἀναγκαῖόν σοι
δοκεῖ δίκαιον εἶναι πᾶν τὸ ὅσιον.   5

ΕΥΘ. Ἔμοιγε.

ΣΩ. Ἆρ᾽ οὖν καὶ πᾶν τὸ δίκαιον ὅσιον; ἢ τὸ μὲν ὅσιον
πᾶν δίκαιον, τὸ δὲ δίκαιον οὐ πᾶν ὅσιον, ἀλλὰ τὸ μὲν αὐτοῦ   12a
ὅσιον, τὸ δέ τι καὶ ἄλλο;

ΕΥΘ. Οὐχ ἕπομαι, ὦ Σώκρατες, τοῖς λεγομένοις.

ΣΩ. Καὶ μὴν νεώτερός γέ μου εἶ οὐκ ἔλαττον ἢ ὅσῳ
σοφώτερος· ἀλλ᾽, ὃ λέγω, τρυφᾷς ὑπὸ πλούτου τῆς σοφίας.   5
ἀλλ᾽, ὦ μακάριε, σύντεινε σαυτόν· καὶ γὰρ οὐδὲ χαλεπὸν
κατανοῆσαι ὃ λέγω. λέγω γὰρ δὴ τὸ ἐναντίον ἢ ὁ ποιητὴς
ἐποίησεν ὁ ποιήσας—
    Ζῆνα δὲ τὸν ἔρξαντα καὶ ὃς τάδε πάντ᾽ ἐφύτευσεν
    οὐκ ἐθέλει νεικεῖν· ἵνα γὰρ δέος ἔνθα καὶ αἰδώς.   b
ἐγὼ οὖν τούτῳ διαφέρομαι τῷ ποιητῇ. εἴπω σοι ὅπῃ;

ΕΥΘ. Πάνυ γε.

ΣΩ. Οὐ δοκεῖ μοι εἶναι "ἵνα δέος ἔνθα καὶ αἰδώς"·
πολλοὶ γάρ μοι δοκοῦσι καὶ νόσους καὶ πενίας καὶ ἄλλα   5
πολλὰ τοιαῦτα δεδιότες δεδιέναι μέν, αἰδεῖσθαι δὲ μηδὲν
ταῦτα ἃ δεδίασιν· οὐ καὶ σοὶ δοκεῖ;

ΕΥΘ. Πάνυ γε.

ΣΩ. Ἀλλ᾽ ἵνα γε αἰδὼς ἔνθα καὶ δέος εἶναι· ἐπεὶ ἔστιν
ὅστις αἰδούμενός τι πρᾶγμα καὶ αἰσχυνόμενος οὐ πεφόβηταί   10
τε καὶ δέδοικεν ἅμα δόξαν πονηρίας;   c

ΕΥΘ. Δέδοικε μὲν οὖν.

ΣΩ. Οὐκ ἄρ᾽ ὀρθῶς ἔχει λέγειν· "ἵνα γὰρ δέος ἔνθα καὶ
αἰδώς," ἀλλ᾽ ἵνα μὲν αἰδὼς ἔνθα καὶ δέος, οὐ μέντοι ἵνα γε
δέος πανταχοῦ αἰδώς· ἐπὶ πλέον γὰρ οἶμαι δέος αἰδοῦς.   5

μόριον γὰρ αἰδὼς δέους ὥσπερ ἀριθμοῦ περιττόν, ὥστε
οὐχ ἵναπερ ἀριθμὸς ἔνθα καὶ περιττόν, ἵνα δὲ περιττὸν ἔνθα
καὶ ἀριθμός. ἔπῃ γάρ που νῦν γε;

ΕΥΘ. Πάνυ γε.

ΣΩ. Τὸ τοιοῦτον τοίνυν καὶ ἐκεῖ λέγων ἠρώτων· ἆρα   10
ἵνα δίκαιον ἔνθα καὶ ὅσιον; ἢ ἵνα μὲν ὅσιον ἔνθα καὶ   d
δίκαιον, ἵνα δὲ δίκαιον οὐ πανταχοῦ ὅσιον· μόριον γὰρ τοῦ
δικαίου τὸ ὅσιον; οὕτω φῶμεν ἢ ἄλλως σοι δοκεῖ;

ΕΥΘ. Οὔκ, ἀλλ᾽ οὕτω. φαίνῃ γάρ μοι ὀρθῶς λέγειν.

ΣΩ. Ὅρα δὴ τὸ μετὰ τοῦτο. εἰ γὰρ μέρος τὸ ὅσιον τοῦ   5
δικαίου, δεῖ δὴ ἡμᾶς, ὡς ἔοικεν, ἐξευρεῖν τὸ ποῖον μέρος
ἂν εἴη τοῦ δικαίου τὸ ὅσιον. εἰ μὲν οὖν σύ με ἠρώτας τι τῶν
νυνδή, οἷον ποῖον μέρος ἐστὶν ἀριθμοῦ τὸ ἄρτιον καὶ τίς ὢν
τυγχάνει οὗτος ὁ ἀριθμός, εἶπον ἂν ὅτι ὃς ἂν μὴ σκαληνὸς
ᾖ ἀλλ᾽ ἰσοσκελής· ἢ οὐ δοκεῖ σοι;   10

ΕΥΘ. Ἔμοιγε.

ΣΩ. Πειρῶ δὴ καὶ σὺ ἐμὲ οὕτω διδάξαι τὸ ποῖον μέρος   e
τοῦ δικαίου ὅσιόν ἐστιν, ἵνα καὶ Μελήτῳ λέγωμεν μηκέθ᾽
ἡμᾶς ἀδικεῖν μηδὲ ἀσεβείας γράφεσθαι, ὡς ἱκανῶς ἤδη
παρὰ σοῦ μεμαθηκότας τά τε εὐσεβῆ καὶ ὅσια καὶ τὰ μή.   5

ΕΥΘ. Τοῦτο τοίνυν ἔμοιγε δοκεῖ, ὦ Σώκρατες, τὸ
μέρος τοῦ δικαίου εἶναι εὐσεβές τε καὶ ὅσιον, τὸ περὶ τὴν
τῶν θεῶν θεραπείαν, τὸ δὲ περὶ τὴν τῶν ἀνθρώπων τὸ
λοιπὸν εἶναι τοῦ δικαίου μέρος.

ΣΩ. Καὶ καλῶς γέ μοι, ὦ Εὐθύφρων, φαίνῃ λέγειν·
ἀλλὰ σμικροῦ τινος ἔτι ἐνδεής εἰμι. τὴν γὰρ θεραπείαν   13a
οὔπω συνίημι ἥντινα ὀνομάζεις. οὐ γάρ που λέγεις γε,
οἷαίπερ καὶ αἱ περὶ τὰ ἄλλα θεραπεῖαί εἰσιν, τοιαύτην καὶ
περὶ θεούς· λέγομεν γάρ που—οἷόν φαμεν, ἵππους οὐ πᾶς
ἐπίσταται θεραπεύειν ἀλλὰ ὁ ἱππικός· ἢ γάρ;   5

ΕΥΘ. Πάνυ γε.

ΣΩ. Ἡ γάρ που ἱππικὴ ἵππων θεραπεία.

ΕΥΘ. Ναί.

ΣΩ. Οὐδέ γε κύνας πᾶς ἐπίσταται θεραπεύειν ἀλλὰ
ὁ κυνηγετικός.   10

ΕΥΘ. Οὕτω.

ΣΩ. Ἡ γάρ που κυνηγετικὴ κυνῶν θεραπεία.

ΕΥΘ. Ναί.   **b**

ΣΩ. Ἡ δέ γε βοηλατικὴ βοῶν.

ΕΥΘ. Πάνυ γε.

ΣΩ. Ἡ δὲ δὴ ὁσιότης τε καὶ εὐσέβεια θεῶν, ὦ
Εὐθύφρων; οὕτω λέγεις;   5

ΕΥΘ. Ἔγωγε.

ΣΩ. Οὐκοῦν θεραπεία γε πᾶσα ταὐτὸν διαπράττεται;
οἷον τοιόνδε· ἐπ' ἀγαθῷ τινί ἐστι καὶ ὠφελίᾳ τοῦ θεραπευομένου,
ὥσπερ ὁρᾷς δὴ ὅτι οἱ ἵπποι ὑπὸ τῆς ἱππικῆς
θεραπευόμενοι ὠφελοῦνται καὶ βελτίους γίγνονται· ἢ οὐ   10
δοκοῦσί σοι;

ΕΥΘ. Ἔμοιγε.

ΣΩ. Καὶ οἱ κύνες γέ που ὑπὸ τῆς κυνηγετικῆς, καὶ οἱ
βόες ὑπὸ τῆς βοηλατικῆς, καὶ τἆλλα πάντα ὡσαύτως· ἢ ἐπὶ   **c**
βλάβῃ οἴει τοῦ θεραπευομένου τὴν θεραπείαν εἶναι;

ΕΥΘ. Μὰ Δί' οὐκ ἔγωγε.

ΣΩ. Ἀλλ' ἐπ' ὠφελίᾳ;

ΕΥΘ. Πῶς δ' οὔ;   5

ΣΩ. Ἦ οὖν καὶ ἡ ὁσιότης, θεραπεία οὖσα θεῶν, ὠφελία
τέ ἐστι θεῶν καὶ βελτίους τοὺς θεοὺς ποιεῖ; καὶ σὺ τοῦτο
συγχωρήσαις ἄν, ὡς ἐπειδάν τι ὅσιον ποιῇς, βελτίω τινὰ
τῶν θεῶν ἀπεργάζῃ;

ΕΥΘ. Μὰ Δί᾽ οὐκ ἔγωγε.   10

ΣΩ. Οὐδὲ γὰρ ἐγώ, ὦ Εὐθύφρων, οἶμαί σε τοῦτο
λέγειν—πολλοῦ καὶ δέω—ἀλλὰ τούτου δὴ ἕνεκα καὶ
ἀνηρόμην τίνα ποτὲ λέγοις τὴν θεραπείαν τῶν θεῶν, οὐχ   d
ἡγούμενός σε τοιαύτην λέγειν.

ΕΥΘ. Καὶ ὀρθῶς γε, ὦ Σώκρατες· οὐ γὰρ τοιαύτην λέγω.

ΣΩ. Εἶεν· ἀλλὰ τίς δὴ θεῶν θεραπεία εἴη ἂν ἡ ὁσιότης;   5

ΕΥΘ. Ἥπερ, ὦ Σώκρατες, οἱ δοῦλοι τοὺς δεσπότας
θεραπεύουσιν.

ΣΩ. Μανθάνω· ὑπηρετική τις ἄν, ὡς ἔοικεν, εἴη θεοῖς.

ΕΥΘ. Πάνυ μὲν οὖν.

ΣΩ. Ἔχοις ἂν οὖν εἰπεῖν ἡ ἰατροῖς ὑπηρετικὴ εἰς τίνος   10
ἔργου ἀπεργασίαν τυγχάνει οὖσα ὑπηρετική; οὐκ εἰς
ὑγιείας οἴει;

ΕΥΘ. Ἔγωγε.

ΣΩ. Τί δὲ ἡ ναυπηγοῖς ὑπηρετική; εἰς τίνος ἔργου   e
ἀπεργασίαν ὑπηρετική ἐστιν;

ΕΥΘ. Δῆλον ὅτι, ὦ Σώκρατες, εἰς πλοίου.

ΣΩ. Καὶ ἡ οἰκοδόμοις γέ που εἰς οἰκίας;

ΕΥΘ. Ναί.   5

ΣΩ. Εἰπὲ δή, ὦ ἄριστε· ἡ δὲ θεοῖς ὑπηρετικὴ εἰς τίνος
ἔργου ἀπεργασίαν ὑπηρετικὴ ἂν εἴη; δῆλον γὰρ ὅτι σὺ
οἶσθα, ἐπειδήπερ τά γε θεῖα κάλλιστα φὴς εἰδέναι
ἀνθρώπων.

ΕΥΘ. Καὶ ἀληθῆ γε λέγω, ὦ Σώκρατες.   10

ΣΩ.   Εἰπὲ δὴ πρὸς Διὸς τί ποτέ ἐστιν ἐκεῖνο τὸ
πάγκαλον ἔργον ὃ οἱ θεοὶ ἀπεργάζονται ἡμῖν ὑπηρέταις
χρώμενοι;

ΕΥΘ.   Πολλὰ καὶ καλά, ὦ Σώκρατες.   **14a**

ΣΩ.   Καὶ γὰρ οἱ στρατηγοί, ὦ φίλε· ἀλλ' ὅμως τὸ
κεφάλαιον αὐτῶν ῥᾳδίως ἂν εἴποις, ὅτι νίκην ἐν τῷ
πολέμῳ ἀπεργάζονται· ἢ οὔ;

ΕΥΘ.   Πῶς δ' οὔ;

ΣΩ.   Πολλὰ δέ γ', οἶμαι, καὶ καλὰ καὶ οἱ γεωργοί· ἀλλ'   5
ὅμως τὸ κεφάλαιον αὐτῶν ἐστιν τῆς ἀπεργασίας ἡ ἐκ τῆς
γῆς τροφή.

ΕΥΘ.   Πάνυ γε.

ΣΩ.   Τί δὲ δὴ τῶν πολλῶν καὶ καλῶν ἃ οἱ θεοὶ ἀπεργάζονται;
τί τὸ κεφάλαιόν ἐστι τῆς ἐργασίας;   10

ΕΥΘ.   Καὶ ὀλίγον σοι πρότερον εἶπον, ὦ Σώκρατες, ὅτι
πλείονος ἔργου ἐστὶν ἀκριβῶς πάντα ταῦτα ὡς ἔχει μαθεῖν·   **b**
τόδε μέντοι σοι ἁπλῶς λέγω, ὅτι ἐὰν μὲν κεχαρισμένα τις
ἐπίστηται τοῖς θεοῖς λέγειν τε καὶ πράττειν εὐχόμενός τε
καὶ θύων, ταῦτ' ἔστι τὰ ὅσια, καὶ σῴζει τὰ τοιαῦτα τούς τε
ἰδίους οἴκους καὶ τὰ κοινὰ τῶν πόλεων· τὰ δ' ἐναντία τῶν   5
κεχαρισμένων ἀσεβῆ, ἃ δὴ καὶ ἀνατρέπει ἅπαντα καὶ ἀπόλλυσιν.

ΣΩ.   Ἦ πολύ μοι διὰ βραχυτέρων, ὦ Εὐθύφρων, εἰ
ἐβούλου, εἶπες ἂν τὸ κεφάλαιον ὧν ἠρώτων· ἀλλὰ γὰρ οὐ
πρόθυμός με εἶ διδάξαι—δῆλος εἶ. καὶ γὰρ νῦν ἐπειδὴ ἐπ'   **c**
αὐτῷ ἦσθα ἀπετράπου· ὃ εἰ ἀπεκρίνω, ἱκανῶς ἂν ἤδη
παρὰ σοῦ τὴν ὁσιότητα ἐμεμαθήκη. νῦν δὲ ἀνάγκη γὰρ τὸν
ἐρωτῶντα τῷ ἐρωτωμένῳ ἀκολουθεῖν ὅπῃ ἂν ἐκεῖνος
ὑπάγῃ, τί δὴ αὖ λέγεις τὸ ὅσιον εἶναι καὶ τὴν ὁσιότητα;   5
οὐχὶ ἐπιστήμην τινὰ τοῦ θύειν τε καὶ εὔχεσθαι;

ΕΥΘ. Ἔγωγε.

ΣΩ. Οὐκοῦν τὸ θύειν δωρεῖσθαί ἐστι τοῖς θεοῖς, τὸ δ᾽
εὔχεσθαι αἰτεῖν τοὺς θεούς;

ΕΥΘ. Καὶ μάλα, ὦ Σώκρατες. 10

ΣΩ. Ἐπιστήμη ἄρα αἰτήσεως καὶ δόσεως θεοῖς ὁσιότης d
ἂν εἴη ἐκ τούτου τοῦ λόγου.

ΕΥΘ. Πάνυ καλῶς, ὦ Σώκρατες, συνῆκας ὃ εἶπον.

ΣΩ. Ἐπιθυμητὴς γάρ εἰμι, ὦ φίλε, τῆς σῆς σοφίας καὶ
προσέχω τὸν νοῦν αὐτῇ, ὥστε οὐ χαμαὶ πεσεῖται ὅτι ἂν 5
εἴπῃς. ἀλλά μοι λέξον τίς αὕτη ἡ ὑπηρεσία ἐστὶ τοῖς θεοῖς;
αἰτεῖν τε φῂς αὐτοὺς καὶ διδόναι ἐκείνοις;

ΕΥΘ. Ἔγωγε.

ΣΩ. Ἆρ᾽ οὖν οὐ τό γε ὀρθῶς αἰτεῖν ἂν εἴη ὧν δεόμεθα
παρ᾽ ἐκείνων, ταῦτα αὐτοὺς αἰτεῖν; 10

ΕΥΘ. Ἀλλὰ τί;

ΣΩ. Καὶ αὖ τὸ διδόναι ὀρθῶς, ὧν ἐκεῖνοι τυγχάνουσιν e
δεόμενοι παρ᾽ ἡμῶν, ταῦτα ἐκείνοις αὖ ἀντιδωρεῖσθαι; οὐ
γάρ που τεχνικόν γ᾽ ἂν εἴη δωροφορεῖν διδόντα τῳ ταῦτα
ὧν οὐδὲν δεῖται.

ΕΥΘ. Ἀληθῆ λέγεις, ὦ Σώκρατες. 5

ΣΩ. Ἐμπορικὴ ἄρα τις ἂν εἴη, ὦ Εὐθύφρων, τέχνη ἡ
ὁσιότης θεοῖς καὶ ἀνθρώποις παρ᾽ ἀλλήλων.

ΕΥΘ. Ἐμπορική, εἰ οὕτως ἥδιόν σοι ὀνομάζειν.

ΣΩ. Ἀλλ᾽ οὐδὲν ἥδιον ἔμοιγε, εἰ μὴ τυγχάνει ἀληθὲς ὄν.
φράσον δέ μοι, τίς ἡ ὠφελία τοῖς θεοῖς τυγχάνει οὖσα ἀπὸ 10
τῶν δώρων ὧν παρ᾽ ἡμῶν λαμβάνουσιν; ἃ μὲν γὰρ διδόασι
παντὶ δῆλον· οὐδὲν γὰρ ἡμῖν ἐστιν ἀγαθὸν ὅτι ἂν μὴ ἐκεῖνοι **15a**
δῶσιν. ἃ δὲ παρ᾽ ἡμῶν λαμβάνουσιν, τί ὠφελοῦνται; ἢ

τοσοῦτον αὐτῶν πλεονεκτοῦμεν κατὰ τὴν ἐμπορίαν, ὥστε
πάντα τὰ ἀγαθὰ παρ' αὐτῶν λαμβάνομεν, ἐκεῖνοι δὲ παρ'
ἡμῶν οὐδέν;   5

ΕΥΘ. Ἀλλ' οἴει, ὦ Σώκρατες, τοὺς θεοὺς ὠφελεῖσθαι
ἀπὸ τούτων ἃ παρ' ἡμῶν λαμβάνουσιν;

ΣΩ. Ἀλλὰ τί δήποτ' ἂν εἴη ταῦτα, ὦ Εὐθύφρων, τὰ παρ'
ἡμῶν δῶρα τοῖς θεοῖς;

ΕΥΘ. Τί δ' οἴει ἄλλο ἢ τιμή τε καὶ γέρα καί, ὅπερ ἐγὼ   10
ἄρτι ἔλεγον, χάρις;

ΣΩ. Κεχαρισμένον ἄρα ἐστίν, ὦ Εὐθύφρων, τὸ ὅσιον,   **b**
ἀλλ' οὐχὶ ὠφέλιμον οὐδὲ φίλον τοῖς θεοῖς;

ΕΥΘ. Οἶμαι ἔγωγε πάντων γε μάλιστα φίλον.

ΣΩ. Τοῦτο ἄρ' ἐστὶν αὖ, ὡς ἔοικε, τὸ ὅσιον, τὸ τοῖς
θεοῖς φίλον.   5

ΕΥΘ. Μάλιστά γε.

ΣΩ. Θαυμάσῃ οὖν ταῦτα λέγων ἐὰν σοι οἱ λόγοι
φαίνωνται μὴ μένοντες ἀλλὰ βαδίζοντες, καὶ ἐμὲ αἰτιάσῃ
τὸν Δαίδαλον βαδίζοντας αὐτοὺς ποιεῖν, αὐτὸς ὢν πολύ γε
τεχνικώτερος τοῦ Δαιδάλου καὶ κύκλῳ περιιόντα ποιῶν; ἢ   10
οὐκ αἰσθάνῃ ὅτι ὁ λόγος ἡμῖν περιελθὼν πάλιν εἰς ταὐτὸν
ἥκει; μέμνησαι γάρ που ὅτι ἐν τῷ πρόσθεν τό τε ὅσιον   **c**
καὶ τὸ θεοφιλὲς οὐ ταὐτὸν ἡμῖν ἐφάνη ἀλλ' ἕτερα
ἀλλήλων· ἢ οὐ μέμνησαι;

ΕΥΘ. Ἔγωγε.

ΣΩ. Νῦν οὖν οὐκ ἐννοεῖς ὅτι τὸ τοῖς θεοῖς φίλον φῂς   5
ὅσιον εἶναι; τοῦτο δ' ἄλλο τι ἢ θεοφιλὲς γίγνεται; ἢ οὔ;

ΕΥΘ. Πάνυ γε.

ΣΩ. Οὐκοῦν ἢ ἄρτι οὐ καλῶς ὡμολογοῦμεν, ἢ εἰ τότε
καλῶς, νῦν οὐκ ὀρθῶς τιθέμεθα.

ΕΥΘ. Ἔοικεν.

ΣΩ. Ἐξ ἀρχῆς ἄρα ἡμῖν πάλιν σκεπτέον τί ἐστι τὸ
ὅσιον, ὡς ἐγὼ πρὶν ἂν μάθω ἑκὼν εἶναι οὐκ ἀποδειλιάσω.
ἀλλὰ μή με ἀτιμάσῃς ἀλλὰ παντὶ τρόπῳ προσσχὼν τὸν   **d**
νοῦν ὅτι μάλιστα νῦν εἰπὲ τὴν ἀλήθειαν· οἶσθα γὰρ εἴπερ τις
ἄλλος ἀνθρώπων, καὶ οὐκ ἀφετέος εἶ ὥσπερ ὁ Πρωτεὺς
πρὶν ἂν εἴπῃς. εἰ γὰρ μὴ ᾔδησθα σαφῶς τό τε ὅσιον καὶ τὸ
ἀνόσιον, οὐκ ἔστιν ὅπως ἄν ποτε ἐπεχείρησας ὑπὲρ ἀνδρὸς   5
θητὸς ἄνδρα πρεσβύτην πατέρα διωκάθειν φόνου, ἀλλὰ
καὶ τοὺς θεοὺς ἂν ἔδεισας παρακινδυνεύειν μὴ οὐκ ὀρθῶς
αὐτὸ ποιήσοις, καὶ τοὺς ἀνθρώπους ᾐσχύνθης· νῦν δὲ εὖ
οἶδα ὅτι σαφῶς οἴει εἰδέναι τό τε ὅσιον καὶ μή. εἰπὲ οὖν, ὦ   **e**
βέλτιστε Εὐθύφρων, καὶ μὴ ἀποκρύψῃ ὅτι αὐτὸ ἡγῇ.

ΕΥΘ. Εἰς αὖθις τοίνυν, ὦ Σώκρατες· νῦν γὰρ σπεύδω
ποι, καί μοι ὥρα ἀπιέναι.

ΣΩ. Οἶα ποιεῖς, ὦ ἑταῖρε. ἀπ' ἐλπίδος με καταβαλὼν   5
μεγάλης ἀπέρχῃ ἣν εἶχον, ὡς παρὰ σοῦ μαθὼν τά τε ὅσια
καὶ μὴ καὶ τῆς πρὸς Μέλητον γραφῆς ἀπαλλάξομαι, ἐνδειξάμενος   **16a**
ἐκείνῳ ὅτι σοφὸς ἤδη παρ' Εὐθύφρονος τὰ θεῖα
γέγονα καὶ ὅτι οὐκέτι ὑπ' ἀγνοίας αὐτοσχεδιάζω οὐδὲ
καινοτομῶ περὶ αὐτά, καὶ δὴ καὶ τὸν ἄλλον βίον ὅτι
ἄμεινον βιωσοίμην.

Commentary

Scene: Outside the Royal Stoa, in the northwest corner of the Athenian agora, 399 BCE.

1   **ΕΥΘΥΦΡΩΝ:** Euthyphro (*PA* 5564; Nails 2002, 152–53) is an Athenian citizen from the deme of Prospalta. In the present conversation, he claims to have spent time on the Cycladic island of Naxos, where his family farmed. Incidents that occurred there have brought him to the office of the archon basileus to prosecute Euthyphro's father for murder (see the introduction herein). Diogenes Laertius (2.29) says that as a result of the conversation dramatized here, the historical Euthyphro decided not to continue the prosecution of his father, although an anecdote like this probably has its origin in a source eager to portray Socrates as sympathetic to Athenian social norms (for a sample of such anecdotes, see Riginos 1976).

There is no mention of Euthyphro in contemporary sources outside of Plato's dialogues, where he appears in the present work and is mentioned in *Cratylus.* There is no reason to believe that he is simply fictional, however. Characters in Plato are generally historical individuals, and the failure of Euthyphro (and perhaps Callicles of *Gorgias*) to appear elsewhere in the historic record is probably due to chance. The Euthyphro of this dialogue claims to have expertise in religious matters and to use his skill to advise his fellow citizens in the *ecclesia* (3c). He is called a *mantis* (seer) by Socrates, a title that Euthyphro does not contest (3e). He also regards himself as an expert about the gods (5e–6a), an assumption that provides the basis for his claim to know about holiness, expressed variously in the dialogue as τὸ ὅσιον, τὰ ὅσια, and ἡ ὁσιότης. This pretended expertise appears consistent with the representation of him in Plato's *Cratylus,* where Socrates mentions Euthyphro's opinions about the significance of divine names and related concepts (396d). For a reconstruction of the social milieu of someone like Euthyphro in the context of the fascinating document known as the Derveni papyrus, see Kahn 1997.

ΣΩΚΡΑΤΗΣ: Socrates (469–399 BCE; *PA* 13101) is from Alopeke, a large deme near the southeast slope of the acropolis. He is the main character of this and numerous other Platonic dialogues. The historical Socrates was apparently an altogether singular individual, but he is known almost entirely through the writings of Plato and Xenophon, who memorialized his unique conversational style, and from the satirical portrait of Aristophanes, whose *Clouds* (423 BCE, later revised) represented Socrates as the leader of a school dedicated to untraditional forms of inquiry, like his attempt to measure the size of a flea's foot (*Nu.* 149–52). Socrates appears in the work of other comic writers as well (see Platter 2014). He is both a part of elite society and an outlier. Many of his interlocutors, such as Nicias, Callias, and Alcibiades, are very prominent. Unlike them, however, Socrates is not a wealthy man (*Ap.* 31c—all references to the *Apology* refer to the work of Plato unless otherwise noted). Xenophon (*Oec.* 2.3) has Socrates list the value of his property at five minas, or five hundred drachmas, a fact that does not seem to concern Socrates (see also X. *Mem.* 1.3.5). Indeed, at *Ap.* 30b he maintains that excellence (ἀρετή) does not come from money (τὰ χρήματα) but that the reverse is true (or, perhaps, that through excellence money becomes good). This attitude puts Socrates squarely in opposition to Athenian attitudes expressed in Pericles' Funeral Oration (Th. 2.40): καὶ τὸ πένεσθαι οὐχ ὁμολογεῖν τινὶ αἰσχρόν, ἀλλὰ μὴ διαφεύγειν ἔργῳ αἴσχιον, "It is not shameful for a man to admit that he is poor but very shameful not to attempt to escape it by his actions."

Socrates also seems to reinterpret the cultural norms of sexual behavior. He is appreciative of male physical beauty and nearly swoons after looking down the cloak of young Charmides (*Chrm.* 155d), but he disdains acting on those desires and channels much of his eroticism into a desire for the Beautiful (see, e.g., the speech of Diotima at *Smp.* 210a–211e). A particularly striking depiction of this quality comes from the speech in which Plato has Alcibiades describe his unsuccessful attempt to seduce Socrates (*Smp.* 217; see also X. *Mem.* 1.3.8–13). All this erotic interest stands in ironic contrast to the fact that Socrates is famous for his ugliness, a quality to which the Platonic dialogues often refer. In the speech mentioned above, Alcibiades compares the face of Socrates to that of a satyr but also says that Socrates' physical ugliness is overwhelmed by his inner beauty (*Smp.* 215b).

Equally striking about Socrates is his unquenchable thirst for conversation. Numerous dialogues represent him as poised to continue the conversation longer than anyone else. In the *Symposium*, which takes place at the home of the tragic playwright Agathon, Socrates is the last one awake at the conclusion of the all-night party (223d). In *Euthyphro*, too, the conversation ends only because Euthyphro suddenly remembers another appointment and declines to begin a new inquiry into the holy (15e3).

2a1   Τί νεώτερον . . . γέγονεν: Not "What's new?" but "Why the change?"
(from the Lyceum to the Royal Stoa). In Greek, the idea of novelty frequently
carries a negative sense (d'Angour 2011). See comm. on 12a4. Compare Plato,
Rep. 424b: τὸ μὴ νεωτερίζειν περὶ γυμναστικήν τε καὶ μουσικὴν παρὰ τὴν
τάξιν, "[they must be watchful about] innovating in gymnastics and music
in a way contrary to the established order." See also the characterization
of Socrates' accuser Meletus as νέος τις (*Euthphr.* 2b8). The strangeness of
Socrates' present legal situation is not exaggerated. He says in the *Apology*, νῦν
ἐγὼ πρῶτον ἐπὶ δικαστήριον ἀναβέβηκα, ἔτη γεγονὼς ἑβδομήκοντα, "I have
entered court now for the first time at the age of seventy" (17d2). ὅτι: "since."

2a1–a2   ἐν Λυκείῳ: The Lyceum, probably named for the presence of a
shrine to Apollo Lyceus, was a public gymnasium located outside the city
walls of Athens in the vicinity of the Ilissos River (see Travlos 1971, 289–91,
345). Gymnasiums were frequented by men and boys of all ages. They offered
outdoor exercise space and training areas, as well as space for relaxation and
conversation. For the range of activities in these spaces, see Forbes 1945.
Gymnasiums figure prominently in the Platonic dialogues. The conversation
reported in *Euthydemus* takes place in the Lyceum. In *Lysis*, Socrates is
on his way to the Lyceum from the Academy (a gymnasium where Plato's
school, discussed in the introduction herein, would be located later) when
he is persuaded to join another conversation (203a). Socrates also goes to
the Lyceum at the end of the *Symposium* (223d). **διατριβάς:** "conversations."
The word also means "pastimes" and refers to spending or wasting time
generally, but in Plato διατριβή and διατρίβειν are virtually synonymous
with the philosophical conversations of Socrates (e.g., *Chrm.* 153a3; *Ap.*
29c8, 37c8; *Grg.* 484e2). This usage may reflect the fact that the historical
Socrates self-deprecatingly referred to his conversations as "pastimes." If this
is true, Euthyphro's use of the word shows that he is sufficiently familiar with
Socrates and his circle to know some of their lingo. The use of διατριβαί to
mean "conversations" is common in Isocrates, but the sense is already present
in Sophocles, fr. 479 Radt: διατριβὰς σοφωτάτας. **διατρίβεις:** Euthyphro's
bantering remark plays on the two senses of διατριβή mentioned above.
The agora, in which the Royal Stoa is located, can be imagined as a place for
wasting time (cf. Ar. *Nu.* 1055; *Ach.* 21), but it can also be a place for Socratic
conversation. In the *Apology*, Socrates asks his judges to excuse him for
speaking just as he does ἐν ἀγορᾷ ἐπὶ τῶν τραπεζῶν, "in the agora at the tables
of the moneychangers" (17c9). There is no evidence for Burnet's view (1924,
87) that Socrates' "serious" conversations took place in the Lyceum and not in
other locations. For example, the *Republic* takes place in a private house, as do
Protagoras and *Gorgias*.

2a2–a3   περὶ τὴν τοῦ βασιλέως στοάν: For the location of the stoa and
the function of the "king," see the introduction herein. οὐ γάρ που: "for I
don't suppose." γάρ is elliptical: "[I ask] because." που is ironic, suggesting
that Euthyphro has considered briefly and then rejected the possibility, on
the basis of his familiarity with Socrates (see also Denniston 1934, 494). The
intimacy Euthyphro presumes is part of Plato's characterization of him but is
not really justified. Euthyphro knows about Socrates' διατριβαί and is familiar
with the *daimonion* (see comm. on 3b5). In addition, we read at *Cra.* 396d
that a man named Euthyphro once filled Socrates' soul with *daimonia sophia*
in regard to the nature of the gods. It seems likely that the same Euthyphro
is intended here (see comm. on 1, s.v. ΕΥΘΥΦΡΩΝ). Still, Euthyphro's
familiarity with Socrates may be partly a mirage. As this dialogue shows,
Euthyphro is unfamiliar with Socrates' style of conversation and unaware
of the accusations Socrates now faces, which would have provoked much
discussion among actual associates of Socrates. καί: "also." σοι γε: "to you
anyway." σοι is here dative of possession, and so is ἐμοί in the next line.

2a4   οὖσα: Translate as infinitive, supplementary participle with τυγχάνω.
πρός τὸν βασιλέα: "before the king," that is, the archon basileus, the
magistrate in charge of Euthyphro's case.

2a5–a6   οὗτοι δὴ Ἀθηναῖοί γε ... δίκην αὐτὴν καλοῦσιν: "Well, the
Athenians, anyway, don't call it a charge" (Denniston 1934, 553, adapted).
τοι ... γε emphasizes the Athenians, as opposed to anyone else who might
have an opinion. δίκην ... γραφήν: Although Socrates clearly means to
imply that a *graphe* is more serious than a *dike*, the distinction is not absolute.
Both words mean "charge," but δίκη is the more general term: all γραφαί are
δίκαι, but not all δίκαι are γραφαί. See Burnet 1924, 88, quoting Pollux 8.41.
Socrates refers to the fact that the specific procedure by which he is being
charged is a *graphe asebeias*—literally, "a charge of disrespect to the gods." See
the introduction herein. For a discussion of the different procedures available,
see MacDowell 1978, 56–66. Such a charge was brought by a private citizen—
in this case, Meletus, assisted by Anytus and Lycon. All three would have
spoken at the trial. For the accusers, see the introduction herein.

2b1   ὡς ἔοικε: Parenthetical: "apparently." γέγραπται: The middle can
take two accusatives to refer to the charge and the person charged.

2b2   ἐκεῖνο: The pronoun refers to the ὡς clause that follows.
καταγνώσομαι: Supply σοῦ. ὡς σὺ ἕτερον: Supply γέγραπται from the
previous line. Again, Euthyphro styles himself as someone who is familiar
with Socrates' habits. See Burnet 1924, 89.

2b3 οὐ γὰρ οὖν: A strong denial (Denniston 1934, 447): "Certainly not!"

2b4 ἀλλὰ σὲ ἄλλος: Supply γέγραπται. Abbreviated rejoinders of this sort are characteristic of Plato's characters, who reproduce the speech styles of everyday life.

2b8 νέος . . . τις: "some young man." τις is indefinite. It has an acute accent because it is followed by the enclitic μοι. For Socrates' dismissive references to Meletus, compare also his description of Meletus in this line as ἀγνώς, "unknown," and τινα . . . Πιτθέα and the careless imprecision of οἷον τετανότριχα, "sort of straight-haired," at 2b10.

2b9 ὡς ἐγῷμαι: Crasis for ὡς ἐγὼ οἶμαι. The phrase is parenthetical. Μέλητον: The chief accuser of Socrates. See the introduction herein. ἔστι: So accented when it appears at the beginning of a sentence.

2b9–b10 τῶν δήμων Πίτθευς: "from the deme Pittheus." τῶν δήμων is a partitive genitive.
εἴ τινα: The accent on εἴ is the result of the enclitic τινα. Compare the accent of τίς at 2b8. εἰ . . . νῷ ἔχεις: "if you remember." νῷ: dative of means.

2b12 Οὐκ ἐννοῶ: "I don't remember." The verb corresponds to νῷ ἔχεις at 2b10.

2c2 ἥντινα; The indirect relative agrees with γραφήν, as does ἀγεννῆ (< ἀγεννής, -ές). Supply a verb of questioning: "[You're asking] what charge?" The construction is colloquial and very common in Plato and Aristophanes. τό . . . ἐγνωκέναι: The articular infinitive with νέον ὄντα as its subject functions as a long noun phrase: "the idea that such a young man has recognized such an important thing is no trivial matter." νέον ὄντα: The participle is concessive. For Greek ideas about novelty, see comm. on 2a1. References to Meletus's youth (see also 2b8) highlight the unstable basis of his accusations. As a νέος himself, he is not in a position to judge whether or not the νέοι are being corrupted (2c4; cf. Ap. 34b; for the correlation between Meletus's age and his supposed wisdom, see also Ap. 25d–e). In the Apology Plato has Socrates include νεότης as a factor contributing to the reckless behavior shown by Meletus in bringing the charges against Socrates: δοκεῖ . . . τὴν γραφὴν ταύτην ὕβρει τινὶ καὶ ἀκολασίᾳ καὶ νεότητι γράψασθαι, "he seems to have brought this charge out of hubris, lack of restraint, and immaturity" (26e–27a). All such references throw an ironic light onto the fact that Socrates is being accused of creating *new* gods (καινούς . . . θεούς, Euthphr. 3b2).

2c4   ὡς φησιν: The parenthetical statement emphasizes that the opinion expressed belongs to Meletus. Socrates pretends to accept the statement at face value and thus praises Meletus for his prodigious wisdom. τίνα τρόπον: adverbial accusative: "how?"

2c5   οἱ διαφθείροντες: The question of who benefits and who corrupts the young people is considered at greater length in the *Apology*, where Meletus is led to assert ridiculously that Socrates is the only person in Athens who corrupts them (25a). The issue of corruption is central both to the case against Socrates (see also *Ap.* 24b9, 33d) and to the dialogue's investigation of piety and impiety. It also links Socrates and Euthyphro, since, by prosecuting his father, Euthyphro, like Meletus, is trying to rid the state of dangerous pollution. κινδυνεύει σοφός τις εἶναι: "he must be a wise man." Socrates pretends to take Meletus seriously. σοφός is a slippery term. Not only is it frequently used to mean "skilled" (cf. σοφίζομαι, "contrive"), but Plato often uses it ironically (as here) or in implied quotation marks to suggest an undeserved reputation for wisdom. In the *Apology* Socrates refers to himself as a σοφός in just this sense when he imagines people who thought of him as the charlatan character from Aristophanes' *Clouds*—that is, as someone who thought himself wise but was not (*Ap.* 18b8, 19c7; see also 38c). This ironic sense of σοφός is programmatic for the *Apology*, especially for Socrates' understanding of the Delphic oracle that no one was wiser than Socrates (21a). Knowing that he was not wise, Socrates set out to test the oracle. He went to several groups of people and concluded that many were not wise at all. Others were wise in one thing but wrongly thought, on such basis, that they were wise in other things as well (21b–22e). In the end, Socrates concluded that the oracle was using him as an example to show that the wisest people were those who, like Socrates, recognized their lack of wisdom (23a–b). In a world where intellectual pretense frequently is mistaken for the real thing, the greatest recognition a person can have is to see the limitations of his or her wisdom. This is harder than it seems, for it requires interrogating oneself ruthlessly to determine if things believed are based on rational beliefs or tired clichés. Plato's Socrates most commonly encounters the latter. Thus, every appearance of the word σοφός and its relatives in the dialogues must be regarded with suspicion. See also comm. on 9b3.

2c6   τὴν ἐμὴν ἀμαθίαν κατιδὼν ὡς διαφθείροντος: "after perceiving my ignorance as [the ignorance] of [me] corrupting." The phrase varies from using the possessive adjective to the possessive genitive (both dependent on ἀμαθίαν).

2c7 **καταγορήσων μου:** Genitive after a verb of accusation, with the future participle expressing purpose. **ὥσπερ πρὸς μητέρα πρὸς τὴν πόλιν:** The comparison is unusual. Meletus, who comes before the city to prosecute Socrates, is compared to a child who comes to his mother to complain about a wrong that has been done to his friends. For πρός plus the accusative in the sense of "before," see comm. on 2a4.

2c8 **τῶν πολιτικῶν:** Probably neuter plural dependent on ἄρχεσθαι: "a political career." Socrates suggests that self-promotion is a part of Meletus's interest in Socrates. For other Platonic characters on the verge of entering political careers, see *Protagoras*, *Menexenus*, and *Alcibiades I*, which also begin with characters on the threshold of public life. It is also possible to take τῶν πολιτικῶν as partitive and masculine ("the only one of the politicians"), but Socrates' insistence on Meletus's youth makes it more difficult to believe that he regards the young man as an established πολιτικός.

2d1 **ὀρθῶς:** = τὸ ὀρθῶς ἄρχεσθαι. "Beginning correctly" is the subject of the sentence.

2d2 **ἐπιμεληθῆναι:** "Have a care for" introduces the ὅπως clause that follows. The verb takes a genitive. The need for careful attention to the self is crucially important in the dialogues. In Plato ἐπιμελέομαι and ἐπιμέλεια frequently appear with strong positive associations. The idea is important because of what it implies about philosophy in the Socratic sense. As a kind of "care," philosophy does not necessarily seek an inspired insight. Instead, it is a continuous practice of (self-)assessment. When Socrates says, in the *Apology*, that "the unexamined life is not worth living" (38a), he refers not to a onetime event but to daily discussions about *arete*. In *Euthyphro*, of course, Socrates does not believe that Meletus's behavior actually constitutes ἐπιμέλεια; Meletus's "care" is merely pretense. In fact, it is possible to see in ἐπιμεληθῆναι a sarcastic play on the name *Meletus*, the "caring" man who does not really care at all. The Socrates of the *Apology* makes the same pun relentlessly (24c8, 24d4, 24d9, 25c3, 26b2). This fact has interesting implications for the interpretation of the dialogues deriving from the order in which they may have been read. If we imagine Plato's readers encountering the *Apology* before *Euthyphro*, the pun points to a line of thought begun in the *Apology* and continuing here. If we imagine *Euthyphro* either written first or encountered first, the pun will be read as a witticism introducing a topos, the significance of which will become clearest after a reading of the *Apology*. Of course, both interpretations would be altered if we were able to discover that the puns on the name of Meletus were part of the speech or practice of the historical

Socrates. For the problems involved in establishing a precise chronology of
the Platonic dialogues, see the introduction herein. For a discussion about
the effect of the taxonomy of the dialogues (and, thus, the order in which
they were read) on larger questions of interpretation, see Poster 1998. ὅτι
ἄριστοι: "as good as possible." γεωργόν: Socrates' analogy is simple, although
it is not clear that this method corresponds to agricultural practice. Just as a
farmer supposedly tends to his young plants first and then to the older ones,
so, according to Socrates' faux-generous characterization, Meletus behaves
sensibly in caring for the young men first. The farming comparison continues
in the next line. εἰκός: Supply ἐστί.

2d4   καὶ τῶν ἄλλων: "also for the others." καὶ δὴ καί: "and in particular."
Denniston 1934, 255.

3a1   ἴσως: Ironic: "maybe." Socrates is trying to imagine a situation
in which the actions of Meletus make sense. ἡμᾶς ἐκκαθαίρει . . . τοὺς
διαφθείροντας: "he clears away . . . those of us who corrupt." The verb also
means "purify," in the sense of clearing away a pollution. In the context of the
vocabulary of corruption that dominates this passage (διαφθείρονται, 2c4;
οἱ διαφθείροντες, 2c5; διαφθείροντος, 2c6; διαφθείροντας, 3a2), the latter
sense predominates. See also Aesch. *Supp.* 263–64 (χθόνα τήνδ' ἐκκαθαίρει
κνωδάλων, "He purifies this land from monsters"), for the connection
of ἐκκαθαίρειν with religious pollution (*miasma*—see Parker 1983). The
agricultural sense of the uncompounded verb has at least one parallel,
however. See X. *Oec.* 20.11: καθαίρειν δὲ δεῖ τὴν γῆν τὸν μέλλοντα σπείρειν,
"It is necessary for someone intending to sow seed to clear the ground." τοὺς
τῶν νέων βλάστας: "the shoots of the young" = "the young shoots."

3a2   ὥς φησιν: Socrates again (see comm. on 2c4) disclaims responsibility
for the motives of Meletus. This phrase is ambiguous, however. What does
Meletus say? It could imply that he is the source of the elaborate farming
comparison. More likely, the phrase picks up διαφθείροντας and recapitulates
the more general charge that Socrates corrupts the youth.

3a3   δῆλον: Supply ἐστί. τῶν πρεσβυτέρων: The genitive is dependent
on ἐπιμεληθείς. πλείστων and μεγίστων ἀγαθῶν are dependent on αἴτιος.
Socrates presumably means the older citizens that are left after people like
Socrates have been weeded out.

3a4–a5   ὥς γε τὸ εἰκὸς συμβῆναι: "as is likely to happen, anyway." The
absolute infinitive construction is similar to ὡς ἐμοὶ δοκεῖν, "as it seems to

me." τὸ εἰκός, "likely," is adverbial.

3a5   ἀρξαμένῳ: The participle refers to Meletus and is dependent on συμβῆναι.

3a6   Βουλοίμην: "if only it were true!" **ὀρρωδῶ:** "shudder." The participle introduces a clause of fearing. The etymology is uncertain (see Beekes 2010, s.v. ὀρρωδέω), but its frequent appearance in Aristophanes (four times) suggests a low stylistic register.

3a7   ἀτεχνῶς: "literally." The word is common in Plato and comedy, as well as in proverbs. As Burnet says (1924, 93), it "emphasizes the essential accuracy of apparently hyperbolic expressions." **δοκεῖ:** The subject is Meletus. **ἀφ᾽ ἑστίας ἄρχεσθαι:** To "begin from the hearth" is to begin from the most basic thing about it and thus do so "utterly." The phrase is proverbial. See Leutsch and Schneidewin 1939, 40, for testimonia. Here, ἑστία probably refers both to private hearths and to the κοινὴ ἑστία, located in the Prytanaeum and functioning as "the symbolic center of the archaic and classical city" (Parker 1996, 26).

3a8   κακουργεῖν: Dependent on ἄρχεσθαι. **ἐπιχείρων ἀδικεῖν σε:** Note the parallelism between this phrase and κακουργεῖν τὴν πόλιν. For Euthyphro, what is bad for Socrates (or for his image of Socrates) is bad for the city.

3a9   τί καὶ ποιοῦντα: "by doing what?" καί is emphatic (Denniston 1934, 312).

3b1   Ἄτοπα . . . ἀκοῦσαι: Socrates answers Euthyphro's question: "[by doing] things that are strange to hear about." **θαυμάσιε:** "you amazing man!" The form of address is unusual. Socrates uses it forty times in the Platonic dialogues, although the vocative does not appear in other authors before Plato. This form of address and such others as μακάριε and βέλτιστε, appearing in the dialogues fifty and forty-two times, respectively, and frequently in comedy (and thus presumed to be colloquial), suggest ironic condescension on the part of Socrates, who does not appear to regard many of his interlocutors as particularly "astonishing," "blessed," or "superlative."

3b2-b3   καινοὺς ποιοῦντα θεούς, τοὺς δ᾽ ἀρχαίους: "creating new gods and not worshipping the old ones." **ποιοῦντα:** Agrees with με. Socrates' summary of the accusation is indirect. "Creating new gods" is made to imply "neglecting established ones" and leading others to follow his example, thus encouraging them to abandon the νομιζόμενα (traditional practices) that distinguish them as Athenians. The charge of corrupting the youth comes up several times in the *Apology*. At 23c we learn that Socrates' young listeners enjoy hearing their elders contradicted. We later hear that they practice his methods at home (33c). The indictment has a different emphasis at *Ap.* 26c, where Meletus is made to insist that Socrates actively intends to corrupt the young, rather than that the corruption is unintentional or follows indirectly from Socrates eccentric religious ideas (Euthyphro's understanding). After a series of exchanges, Meletus declares that Socrates is not merely a religious innovator but a full-blown atheist. Xenophon (*Mem.* 1.2.9–11), however, insists that Socrates did not teach his associated to scorn the established laws and customs of the city.

3b3   **νομίζοντα:** " honor." τοὺς δ᾽ ἀρχαιοὺς οὐ νομίζοντα is similar to the language of the so-called "Diopeithes decree" passed by the Athenian assembly and directed at τοὺς τὰ θεῖα μὴ νομίζοντας, "those who do not honor the gods"—specifically, against the philosopher Anaxagoras, who was Pericles' friend (Plutarch, *Per.* 32). Whether or not the Diopeithes decree was still in effect after the revision of the Athenian law code in 403–402 is still the subject of scholarly discussion (for a summary, see Strycker and Slings 1994, 86–87). The threshold of religious indifference that could reasonably trigger a charge of *asebeia* is uncertain. Each Athenian did not participate in every religious celebration. Euripides' Hippolytus is not represented as a character for our emulation. Nevertheless, his assessment must have been essentially right: ἄλλοισιν ἄλλος θεῶν τε κἀθρώπων μέλει, "Each has his likes, in gods and men alike" (*Hipp.* 104, trans. Kovacs). In addition, Xenophon clearly feels that Socrates' religious observations were not unusual: θύων τε γὰρ φανερὸς ἦν πολλάκις μὲν οἴκοι, πολλάκις δὲ ἐπὶ τῶν κοινῶν τῆς πόλεως βωμῶν, "He was sacrificing often in plain view at home and at the common altars of the city" (*Mem.* 1.2; see also X. *Ap.* 11).

3b5–c5   Euthyphro expresses empathy with Socrates. Their mutual association with divine phenomena opens both of them to the mockery of the uninitiated public. The comparison is strengthened by the characterization of Socrates' *daimonion* as μαντική (*Ap.* 40a), since Euthyphro is also a μάντις. As Adam notes (1890, 42–43), Socrates tacitly rejects Euthyphro's empathy with his reference to ὑμῖν τοῖς μάντεσιν, "you seers" (*Euthphr.* 3e3). The dialogue plays regularly with the tension between the idea that Socrates and Euthyphro are antagonists—Euthyphro's prosecution of his father, involving a younger man prosecuting an older one for impiety, parallels Meletus's prosecution of Socrates—and the idea that Socrates and Euthyphro are oddly related (see, e.g., 11c–d, where each accuses the other of being like the mythological sculptor Daedalus).

3b5   Μανθάνω: "I understand." δαιμόνιον: < δαίμων, "god": "divinity." The diminutive probably suggests Socrates' long familiarity with the experience. In addition, the suffix may reflect Plato's concern to separate Socrates' experience from traditional beliefs about a personal guardian (see, e.g., Hesiod, *WD* 122–24, where after death the Golden Age men become spirits (δαίμονες) described as φύλακες θνητῶν ἀνθρώπων (quoted slightly differently at Plato, *Rep.* 469a). See also Lysias 2.78. The *daimonion* of Socrates is not an invention of Plato (although Plato may have shaped the idea to serve his own philosophical purposes). Xenophon mentions it as well. At *Mem.* 1.1.2 he appears to agree with the assumption of Euthyphro that the charge of bringing in new gods is a covert reference for Socrates' "divine thing"; see also *Ap.* 31d, where Socrates says that Meletus referred mockingly to the *daimonion* (ἐπικωμῳδῶν) in his indictment.

The *daimonion* is an internal experience. Socrates interprets its occurrence (γίγνεσθαι; cf. *Ap.* 31d) as a sign to abandon whatever course of action he intends. It often has a major influence on to whom Socrates talks. At *Phd.* 242b–c Socrates ends a preliminary conversation but decides to continue after the *daimonion*'s intervention. So also, in *Euthydemus*, Socrates describes preparing to leave the Lyceum but being dissuaded from going by an experience of the *daimonion* (272e). The conversation that makes up *Alcibiades I* only takes place because the *daimonion* no longer opposes Socrates' conversation with the young Alcibiades (103a; also 105d). The intervention of the *daimonion* may also have practical effects. In the *Apology* Socrates implies that it prevented him from entering politics and thus running afoul of the city for a while (31d–e). By the same logic that led him to converse with Alcibiades, he concludes in the *Apology* that his conviction is a good thing since the *daimonion* did not prevent him from delivering the speech he was intending to deliver (40a–b).

3b6   καινοτομοῦντος: Literally, "to make a new cut"; metaphorically, "innovate" (cf. Ar. *V.* 876, with the note of Biles and Olson 2016). The idea is repeated at 5a8 and 16a3. The metaphor is derived from attempting to locate a new productive vein in mining (see X. *Vect.* 4.27) but is often connected with antidemocratic political innovation (Ar. *Ec.* 586; A. *Pol.* 1305b40, 1316b19). In view of the dramatic date of *Euthyphro*, set at the time of the democratic restoration after the fall of the Thirty, the metaphor may here be code for a charge of advocating oligarchic views.

3b7 τὰ θεῖα: The generic plural is conceivably an echo of the Diopeithes decree of ca. 432 BCE. The decree, if genuine (it is not mentioned outside of Plutarch, *Per.* 32), supposedly provided for the prosecution of men like the philosopher Anaxagoras (Pericles' friend), on the ground that they were irreligious (εἰσαγγέλλεσθαι τοὺς τὰ θεῖα μὴ νομίζοντας). See also Sophocles, *Oed.* 910; *OC* 1537. The prepositional phrase effects a dramatic transition for Euthyphro, from expressing a mild interest in Socrates' case to talking about himself. See περὶ τῶν θεῶν at *Euthphr.* 3c1.

3b8 διαβαλῶν: Future participle (with ὡς): "to slander [you]." **δή**: Translated only by a rising tone of voice, the particle emphasizes the participle to draw attention to what Denniston (1934, 230) calls "the unworthy . . . motive" of Meletus.

3b9 εὐδιάβολα: "easy to distort." διαβολα repeats with emphasis the idea of διαβαλῶν.

3b9–c2 ἐμοῦ . . . καταγελῶσιν: The hyperbaton is extreme. Having Euthyphro begin with a reference to himself in the genitive, then postponing the verb that governs it for one and a half lines, allows Plato to show Euthyphro's near theatrical interest in keeping as much attention as possible focused on himself.

3c1–c2 προλέγων . . . τὰ μέλλοντα: "prophesying the future." A *mantis* normally would weigh in on the foundation of colonies or on issues of religious ritual. No doubt, there were frequent opportunities to do so. The prominence of oracles at Athens forms the premise of the plot of Aristophanes' *Knights*, where an oracle predicts the rise of a sausage seller to dethrone the demagogue Cleon (represented as a leather tanner). Although oracles are the specific domain of the *chresmologos*, they would also be expected to elicit comment from those specially connected with the service of the gods. Plutarch (*Per.* 6.2) reports that the *mantis* Lampon predicted the victory of Pericles over his rival Thucydides.

3c2 μαινομένου: To predict the future Euthyphro must rely on nonrational forces—or at least on arbitrary interpretation of nonrational phenomena (bird signs, the organs of sacrificial victims, etc.). The appearance of this word here hints at a connection between μαίνομαι and μάντις. For the etymology, see Beekes 2010, s.v. μαίνομαι.

3c3 οὐδέν: Supply ἐστί: "there is nothing."

3c4   φθονοῦσιν: "they resent." That envious resentment is a natural reaction to someone else's abilities or good fortune is a normal fifth-century assumption: ἴσχει τε γὰρ ὄλβος οὐ μείονα φθόνον (Pi. *Pyth.* 11.29). The idea extends to divine and human interaction as well: τὸ θεῖον πᾶν ἐὸν φθονερόν, "Divinity is entirely envious" (Herod. 1.32).

Euthyphro's innocent question about Socrates' unexpected presence at the Royal Stoa has evolved quickly into a vehicle for his own self-praise. He is crucially wrong, however, about the similarity between his situation and that of Socrates, as well as about his assessment of the forces lined up against each of them. At *Ap.* 23a, Socrates tells about the hatred he incurred not just from those whom he refuted but from audience members who expected him to give his own opinion about the subject under discussion. That he did not do so made him appear to put himself above everyone, although he maintains that he behaved thus not out of arrogance but out of a belief that human wisdom is not worth much (23a8). Such a position may have done little to improve his image. Several decades before Socrates' death, Aristophanes had already portrayed him as a man who walked around arrogantly casting his head from side to side: βρενθύει τ' ἐν ταῖσιν ὁδοῖς καὶ τὠφθαλμὼ παραβάλλεις (*Nu.* 362). While Plato represented the aristocratic and antinomian Alcibiades as quoting the Aristophanic line with amusement (*Smp.* 221b), other Athenians may have taken offense at Socrates carrying himself in this way. The aggressive, uncompromising style of Socrates could also have been irksome. Xenophon remarks on it in his *Apology*, where he refers to Socrates' μεγαληγορία (1), which Henderson translates as "cockiness" (Marchent and Todd 2013). The poet Agathon responds to what he perceives as Socrates' ironic effusive praise by accusing Socrates of hubris (*Smp.* 175e8), and Alcibiades characterizes Socrates similarly after failing to seduce him (*Smp.* 219c).

3c4-c5   αὐτῶν . . . ὁμόσε ἰέναι: "come to close quarters [with them]." The pronoun refers to the subject of φθονοῦσιν (3c4), the men who form the juries (for Socrates) and sit in the assembly (for Euthyphro). The phrase is Homeric (*Il.* 13.337), although its appearances at Th. 2.62, Ar. *Ec.* 863, and X. *Cyr.* 3.3.57 suggests that it became a cliché. Euthyphro tells Socrates to confront his critics as though they were enemy soldiers. In so doing, Euthyphro styles himself as a latter-day Homeric hero, a characterization he certainly does not merit. Thus, the phrase stands in ironic contrast to an image Plato creates of Socrates in the *Apology* (28c–d), as a modern Achilles willing to risk death rather than to live shamefully as an ἄχθος ἀρούρης (*Il.* 18.104).

3c6   τὸ μὲν καταγελασθῆναι: Supply ἐστί. Socrates begins his reply as though he were going to contrast (μέν) being laughed at with something like being injured. The syntax shifts, however, from talking about what the Athenians do to considering the kind of person they do it to (ὃν δ᾽ ἂν καὶ ἄλλους οἴωνται ποιεῖν τοιούτους, 3c). As a result, there is no corresponding δέ.

3c8   σφοδρά: "really," taken closely with μέλει. **δεινόν:** "dangerous." In the fifth century, this word derived from δέος, "fear," came to mean "clever" or "skillful" and meant "dangerous" when applied to those clever or skillful enough to make people nervous. For example, Oedipus tells Creon, λέγειν σὺ δεινός ("You are a skilled speaker," S. *OT* 545). At the beginning of the *Apology* (17b), Socrates implies that his accusers have warned the jurors not to be led astray by him, on the ground that he is δεινὸς λέγειν, "a dangerous speaker" (the infinitive is epexegetical). **ἄν:** = ἐάν. **μή:** Introduces a clause of proviso, for which understand οἴωνται from the previous clause: "provided they do not think he is a teacher [διδασκαλικόν] of his skill."

3c9–4d1   ὃν δ᾽ ἂν καὶ ἄλλους οἴωνται ποιεῖν τοιούτους: "whomever [object of θυμοῦνται] they think makes others like himself," that is, "dangerous" in the same way that he himself is dangerous.

3d1–d2   ὡς σὺ λέγεις: By emphasizing that Euthyphro attributed the reaction of the Athenians to their *phthonos*, Socrates hints that Euthyphro's diagnosis of the Athenian reaction to Socrates may be incorrect (εἴτε δι ἄλλο τι).

3d3   τούτου ... πέρι: The penultimate accent on the preposition indicates that the object precedes it (anastrophe). Euthyphro has already said that those in the assembly laugh at him as though he were a madman (3c), and he attributed those feelings to resentment and envy (φθόνος). Here, he imagines the possibility that their thoughts about him are far worse.

3d6   διδάσκειν οὐκ ἐθέλειν: There is some incongruity between, on the one hand, the frequency of Euthyphro's presence at the assembly as implied by ὅταν τι λέγω at 3c1) and, on the other, the idea that he has only displayed his wisdom "rarely" (σπάνιον, 3d5). Perhaps Euthyphro has been less active politically than he implies. We will soon learn that he has spent some time away from the city, farming on the island of Naxos. Euthyphro's supposed reluctance to teach is a frequent leitmotif of the dialogue (cf. 3d5, 6d2, 6d10, 6e4, 9a1, 9d9, 11e3, 12e1, 15e2).

3d7   **φιλανθρωπίας:** In contrast to Euthyphro, who speaks rarely in public, Socrates is known to offer himself for questioning to rich and poor men alike (*Ap.* 33a). His φιλανθρωπία is thus very different from the pseudo-φιλανθρωπία that Isocrates (15.133) identifies as a strategy for duping (φενακιζόντας) the masses.

3d8   **ἐκκεχυμένως:** Participle < ἐγχέω: "pour out." Socrates' words are served up like cups of wine for anyone who will listen.

3d9   **προστιθεὶς ἄν:** "I would add [a fee]." The participle replaces a potential optative. Supply μίσθον from the previous line. Unlike the Sophists, Socrates does not charge a fee for instruction (*Ap.* 33a–b). Here he humorously imagines that he would actually pay people to converse with him.

3d10   **μὲν οὖν:** "so, [as I was just now saying]." After the digression on Euthyphro's reticence to speak before the assembly and Socrates' "philanthropic" willingness to talk, μὲν οὖν brings us back to the original topic Socrates introduced at 3c6. This usage of the particle combination is called "resumptive." **καταγελᾶν:** Translate twice, with μου and σεαυτοῦ.

3e1–e2   **παίζοντας . . . γελῶντας:** Supply ἡμᾶς.

3e2   **διαγαγεῖν:** "spend time."

3e3   **μάντεσιν:** The comment is ironic. Seers are regularly mocked in comedy. They do not fare much better in Plato. See *Ap.* 22c; *Men.* 99c; *Ion* 534c–d. Like poets, they act on the basis of inspiration, not rational judgment.

3e5   **κατὰ νοῦν:** "as you think best." **οἶμαι δὲ καὶ ἐμὲ τὴν ἐμήν:** Supply ἀγωνιεῖσθαι for the indirect statement, on the basis of ἀγωνιῇ in the previous clause. Euthyphro turns the conversation back to his own case, which he is dying to talk about.

3e7   **τίς ἡ δίκη:** Socrates' question is polite. He already knows that Euthyphro has a δίκη. **φεύγεις . . . διώκεις:** Technical legal vocabulary describing the behavior of the defendant and the plaintiff, respectively.

4a1   **Ὃν διώκων . . . αὖ δοκῶ μαίνεσθαι:** Euthyphro's reply is riddling and theatrical. He appears to take pleasure in the notoriety his action brings. αὖ may allude to the first mention of madness, μαινομένου (3c2). In both cases, seeming madness is one of the ways by which Euthyphro dramatizes his sense of superiority to the multitude (cf. 5a1, where he is more explicit).

4a2 πετόμενόν τινα διώκεις: Socrates accepts Euthyphro's riddle in a humorous vein and returns the favor, punning on the proverb that means "attempt the impossible," while exploiting the sense of διώκειν as both "pursue" and "prosecute." For the idea, see also Arist. *Met.* 1009b38; A. *Ag.* 394. Euthyphro continues the conceit, also exploiting both senses of διώκειν and pointing ironically to the inappropriateness of "flight" when applied to a man of advanced age like his father.

4a3 δεῖ: Not "it is necessary," but "is lacking." The expression takes a complementary infinitive. The subject of δεῖ is the relative clause (ὅς γε τυγχάνει . . . πρεσβύτης). Euthyphro is still coy about whom he is prosecuting.

4a6 ὁ ἐμὸς πατήρ: Although tragedy and comedy stage conflict between fathers and sons as central to drama, the prospect of a son prosecuting his father is imagined to be shocking. See B. Strauss 1993.

4a9 ἔγκλημα: A summary of the charge. Euthyphro has perhaps just delivered it to the archon basileus. For the procedure see Phillips 2013. τίνος: Genitive of the charge; see also φόνου at 4a10.

4a11 Ἡράκλεις: Exclamation of surprise. Herakles is often called upon as "averter of evils" (ἀλεξίκακος). The two words may appear together or either separately for the sense to be understood. Compare Lucian *Alex.* 4.1; *Gall.* 2.1; schol. on Ar. *Nu.* 1372. The absence of ὦ before the vocative reflects Socrates' surprised reaction (real or feigned) to Euthyphro's revelation.

4a11 ἀγνοεῖται: The verb is impersonal. ὑπὸ τῶν πολλῶν: "by the many." Socrates implies that Euthyphro will have difficulty again when he brings his views to the public. ὅπη ποτὲ ὀρθῶς ἔχει: "how in the world it is right."

4a12–b2 τοῦ ἐπιτυχόντος . . . ἐλαύνοντος: The genitives express traits: "it is not [characteristic] of someone whom you happen to meet [literally, someone who happens to meet you] to do this in a way that is correct [ὀρθῶς αὐτὸ πρᾶξαι], as opposed to all of the ways something could be done incorrectly." In the case of ἐλαύνοντος, the metaphor is from chariot racing: "driving far along in wisdom" (cf. Ar. *Nu.* 25). Socrates assumes ironically that Euthyphro's decision is based on advanced wisdom rather than a carelessly drawn conclusion.

4b3 πόρρω: Euthyphro repeats part of Socrates' "admiring" comment to affirm its (unironic) truth. μέντοι: Denniston's comment on the emphatic use of μέντοι is apt: "μέν denotes [what Euthyphro perceives as] objective certainty, while τοι brings the truth home to another person" (1934, 399). Euthyphro's self-congratulatory tone is strengthened further by the oath: "Quite far along, by Zeus, let me tell you."

4b4 τῶν οἰκείων: These would include family members as well as slaves. ὁ τεθνεώς: "the victim" (literally, "the dead man"). Forms of (ἀπο-)θνῄσκω appear frequently as the passive of ἀποκτείνω (see 9a3; *Ap.* 29d1: ἀποθανῇ, "You will be put to death").

4b5 ἢ δῆλα δή; "or is that obvious?" ἀλλητρίου . . . φόνου: That is, the murder of someone outside the *oikos*.

4b6 ἐπεξῇσθα: ἐπεχέρχομαι takes a dative of the person accused. The imperfect with ἄν indicates a situation counter to fact: "you wouldn't be prosecuting."

4b7 Γέλοιον: Supply ἐστί. διαφέρειν: Dependent on οἴει, as is δεῖν. εἴτε . . . εἴτε: Supply ἐστί. The familial status of the victim is not important, says Euthyphro. The only issue worth considering is whether the killer acted justly or not.

4b9 ἐν δίκη: "justly." Euthyphro's language anticipates his description of Cronus "unjustly" (οὐκ ἐν δίκη) swallowing his children (6a2).

4b10 ἐᾶν . . . ἐπεξιέναι: Dependent on δεῖν. The ἐάνπερ clause that follows refers only to ἐπεξιέναι. It is important to prosecute cases of unjust killing by members of one's own household since eating or engaging in ritual activities with them could allow you to become infected with their μίασμα (see the introduction herein). From someone unrelated, the danger might be substantially less.

4c1 συνέστιος . . . ὁμοτράπεζος: Both words suggest the shared experience that characterizes all members of an *oikos*, with different emphases. συνέστιος refers to private religious activities centered around the hearth, itself synecdochic for the entire household (cf. 3a). ὁμοτράπεζος refers more narrowly to the experience of communal eating around the same table. μίασμα: "defilement" (see the introduction herein). Fear of contagion made it necessary to forbid the polluted person from participating in a variety of communal activities (see Parker 1983, 104–11).

The sentence is unusually convoluted, probably owing to Euthyphro's excitement: "It is funny that you think it matters at all whether the victim is a member of the household or an outsider, but do not think that this alone is necessary to watch out for, whether the one who killed did so justly or not—and if justly, [it is necessary that] you must let him go, but if not, prosecute him, if the killer is someone who shares your hearth and table."

4c1–e2   Euthyphro's story begins at his family's property on the island of Naxos. Although he does not say so, it is generally understood that the family must have been farming as cleruchs, Athenians who retained their citizenship but became colonists on allotted land, in this case after a revolt. Naxos had a history of rebelliousness. It had attempted to secede from the Delian League before being recaptured by Cimon in the mid-460s (Th. 1.98). It was later compelled to accept colonists, who would have helped to ensure political stability (from the point of view of Athens). At the end of the Peloponnesian War in 404, Athens was forced to give up such settlements, giving us a *terminus ante quem* for the crimes described by Euthyphro. Given that the dramatic date of *Euthyphro* is 399, weeks before the trial of Socrates, it is unclear why Euthyphro will have waited at least five years to pursue the case. Various hypotheses have been advanced, but direct evidence is scant, and much remains unclear. Solving this problem does not appear to be key for understanding the dialogue, however. Socrates sees nothing strange in Euthyphro's chronology, and the details of Athenian cleruchies do not play a role in the subsequent conversation.

4c4   πελάτης . . . ἐμός: "my employee." For the term, see the Aristotelian *Ath.* 2.2, where the πελάτης is also called ἑκτήμορος (a tenant who pays one-sixth of each crop to the landowner; see also Rhodes 1993, 90–91). Later usage seems to have been less precise regarding the details of tenancy. The scholia glosses the term simply as "someone working for a wage." For the purposes of the dialogue, the key detail of the man's status is that he is not from the *oikos* of Euthyphro's father (cf. ἀλλότριος at 4b8), although the possessive adjective perhaps suggests that he had a long-standing relationship with the family.

4c5   ἐθήτευεν: < θής, "laborer": "work as a day laborer." Euthyphro does not make it clear if the man was a hired Naxian or someone who accompanied the family from Athens. παροίνησας: "having drunk too much." The verb emphasizes not the physical symptoms of drunkenness but the kind of antisocial behavior that might result from it.

4c6   τῶν οἰκετῶν τινι τῶν ἡμετέρων: The logic of the events has little to do with the rights of the slave. He is the property of the father, and the πελάτης who killed him is therefore responsible for compensating the father for the loss. To ensure that compensation happens, the father ties up the offender and leaves him in a ditch. His decision seems unusually reckless. Does he imagine that no sufficient compensation will be forthcoming and thus (with extraordinary cruelty) assume that justice will take its course— all the while providing cover for himself by making a show of seeking an official opinion on his next course of action (see comm. on 4c9 and 4d1-d2)? **ἀποσφάττει:** The present tense adds a vivid climax to the whole sordid story (cf. also πέμπει at 4c8).

4c7   **ὁ οὖν πατήρ:** The description's fast pace is created by the absence of conjunctions (explanatory asyndeton).

4c8   **τάφρον:** Perhaps used for irrigation, as at *P. Hal.* 1.93 (Egypt, third century). A water course that has been found and is thought to date from the sixth century would have supplied water to the town of Naxos and to arable land along the way. Construction required tunneling through a mountain. See Herodotus 3.60 for a discussion of a tunnel from the same period on nearby Samos (see also Asheri 2007, 455–57). **πέμπει:** The present tense is historical. The optative that follows (χρή > χρείη) is treated as a secondary tense for the purpose of the indirect question.

4c9   **ἐξηγετοῦ:** The exegetes were expounders of unwritten sacred law and custom. They were traditionally from the *genos* of the Eumolpidae, which also was associated prominently with the administration of the Eleusinian Mysteries (cf. *H. Cer.* 475). Why the father thought it was important to consult them before proceeding with a prosecution is not known. Perhaps he was uncertain about the jurisdiction under which the case fell. The murderer of a slave could be prosecuted by the slave's owner under Attic law. Such cases were the responsibility of the archon basileus and were tried in court at the Palladium (*Ath.* 57.3). Not everyone treated the instiution with consumate respect. The superstitious man (δεισιδαίμων) of Theophrastus the Exegete for ritual instruction after the most trivial event—a mouse that has chewed a hole in his sack of barley. (*Ca.* 16.6). It is perfectly possible that the father had no interest in an actual prosecution and that the trip to the exegetes was simply an excuse to delay releasing the murderer (see comm. on 4c6). **ὅτι χρείη ποιεῖν:** "what it was necessary to do." As noted by Burnet (1924, 106), ὅτι χρὴ ποιεῖν appears to be the formula for consulting the exegetes (cf. Demosthenes 47.68: ἦλθον ὡς τοὺς ἐξηγητάς, ἵνα εἰδείην ὅ τι με χρὴ ποιεῖν περὶ τούτων, "I went to the exegetes to find out what I should do").

4d1–d2 τοῦ δεδεμένου ὠλιγώρει τε καὶ ἠμέλει ὡς ἀνδροφόνου καὶ
οὐδὲν ὂν πρᾶγμα, εἰ καὶ ἀποθάνοι: "he gave no thought to and neglected the
bound man since he was a murderer, and since it was not important even if he
should die." οὐδὲν ὂν πρᾶγμα is accusative absolute (Smyth 1956, 2059). The
understanding of Euthyphro's father is that by killing the slave, the worker has
forfeited his right to be treated humanely. ὡς: "on the ground that."

4d4 πρίν . . . ἀφικέσθαι: The timeline is uncertain. Schiedel and Meeks
(2012) estimate the travel time from Naxos to Athens to be from 1.5 to 3.5
days each way, depending on a number of factors, including whether night
travel is included. Thus, an especially speedy messenger could have been
gone for as few as four days. Such calculations cannot take into account how
often such boats sailed, how easy or difficult it may have been to meet with
an exegete, or whether consulting an exegete was the express purpose of the
messenger's trip or only one of a series of errands. Therefore, the real length
of the trip could have been substantially longer, especially if the haste of the
messenger is commensurate with the lackadaisical attitude that Euthyphro's
father showed toward the criminal's well-being (ὠλιγώρει, ἠμέλει). The death
of the *pelates* may well have been a long and painful affair, and it is no small
wonder that Euthyphro was disturbed by it.

4d5–d10 Euthyphro's father and family interpret what happened
differently. Their anger that Euthyphro has brought this prosecution against
his father has three reasons: (1) since he had already committed murder,
the victim deserved no special protection; (2) the father was not the killer,
strictly speaking, since the laborer died of exposure; (3) it is unholy (ἀνόσιον)
for a son to prosecute his father. Euthyphro takes the view that there is no
difference between murder and negligence that leads to death. Therefore,
the pollution caused by the murder must be removed by purification and
prosecution.

  The sentence is difficult, with two parenthetical remarks and a change of
construction. The first part is governed by ἀγανακτεῖ (4d5). After the first
parenthesis (ὥς φασιν ἐκεῖνοι), supply φασιν as the verb introducing the
indirect statement (accusative subject plus infinitive) up through ἐπεξιέναι
(4e1), after which εἰδότες (< οἶδα) agrees with the plural subject of φασιν
(4d7).

4d5 ταῦτα: Equivalent to διὰ ταῦτα: "because of this."

4d7 οὔτε ἀποκτείναντι: The participle agrees with πατρί: "[who is]
neither a man who has killed." οὔτ᾽ εἰ . . . ἀπέκτεινεν: "nor if he had killed."

ὡς φασιν ἐκεῖνοι: "as they [the father and family members] say." Burnet (1924, 105–6) thought that ὥς φασιν ἐκεῖνοι implied some sort of official legal maneuvering that might have delayed the case (see comm. herein on 4c1–e2). Socrates refers later to the legal maneuver of *episkepsis*, "denunciation," wherein a prosecutor might respond to a claim that the prosecution was illegal (*diamarturia*). See comm. on 9a8. Use of this process in the case of Euthyphro's prosecution might mean that a family member challenged Euthyphro's ability to prosecute on behalf of someone not a member of his family. Nothing in this passage directly supports that idea, however. ὅτι μάλιστα: "actually." See also 9c3.

4d7–d8   ὅτι μάλιστα: "actually." See also 9c3.

4d9   δεῖν: Indirect statement after φασιν: "nor is it necessary to worry about a man such as the dead man, who himself was a murderer." ἀνόσιον: τὰ ὅσια are things that the gods require of human beings, which covers a broad range of activities, from observing religious festivals and preserving traditional religious practices (as understood by individuals or by specialists like the exegetes) to respecting one's parents and refraining from crimes of violence. To bring a court case against a parent, which could be considered the antithesis of these cultural norms, could thus be regarded as ἀνόσιον.

    The mention of unholiness makes explicit, for the first time, the principle subject of the dialogue: the process of showing Euthyphro that although his decision to prosecute his father presumes knowledge of holiness (and unholiness), he has no coherent understanding of either.

4e1   ὑόν: The noun functions as the subject of the articular infinitive τό . . . ἐπεξιέναι: "for a son to prosecute his father for murder is unholy." κακῶς εἰδότες: "misunderstanding."

4e2   τὸ θεῖον ὡς ἔχει: = ὡς τὸ θεῖον ἔχει. The construction is proleptic (Smyth 1956, 2182): "how the attitude of the gods [τὸ θεῖον] is related to the holy and the unholy." Compare περὶ τῶν θείων ὅπη ἔχει at 4e5 τοῦ ὁσίου τε πέρι καὶ τοῦ ἀνοσίου: Note the anastrophe of the preposition (marked by the accent moved to the penult).

4e7   ὅπως μή: With the subjunctive, ὅπως μή can introduce a clause describing what may prove to be a fear (Smyth 1956, 2228).

4e8   ἀνόσιον πρᾶγμα: Socrates suggests that Euthyphro's understanding of the holy is flawed. The ensuing conversation will address the issue from a philosophical perspective. Here Socrates appeals to the conventional morality that endorses filial loyalty without equivocation. By that measure, it is always ἀνόσιον for a son to prosecute his father.

4e9   οὐδὲν γὰρ ἄν μου ὄφελος εἴη: "I would be of no use" (literally, "there would be no benefit of me at all").

5a1   τῳ: Contracted form of τινι: "at all." Taken with the genitive of comparison the dative indicates the degree of superiority. Note the self-dramatizing quality produced by Euthyphro's reference to himself in the third person.

5a3–b8   Euthyphro has declared himself to be an expert on divine matters, and Socrates has been accused of crimes against the gods (*asebeia*). Socrates pretends to take their meeting as fortunate and imagines the benefits of becoming Euthyphro's student (5a4; see also 5c5), in hopes of convincing Meletus that he has been reeducated. The joke depends on taking seriously Euthyphro's claim to know περὶ τῶν θείων ὅπη ἔχει, as claiming for himself a special knowledge capable of being taught. The rest of the dialogue will test that claim.

The test goes both ways, however. Although Socrates never claims expert knowledge of the divine, he insists that his practice of interrogating his fellow citizens is λατρεία (service) to Apollo (*Ap.* 23c), the source of the oracle that said that no one was wiser than Socrates. The philosopher had interpreted the oracle to mean that no one was knowledgeable about the gods and that the wisest man was someone who, like Socrates, recognized his ignorance (*Ap.* 23b). Euthyphro's claim to expert knowledge about the gods would offer an implicit challenge to that interpretation, if Socrates were to take Euthyphro seriously enough. Instead, Socrates does not seem to regard Euthyphro very highly and seems amused at Euthyphro's pretensions.

5a3   θαυμάσιε: "you amazing man." The vocative is common in Plato (forty appearances).

5a4   τῆς γραφῆς: The actual trial, not the written charge.

5a5   αὐτὰ ταῦτα: "about these very things" (accusative of respect)—specifically, that the substance of Meletus's charge has been made irrelevant thanks to the tutelage of Euthyphro. προκαλεῖσθαι: "challenge," a technical legal term. A *proklesis* gave the litigant the opportunity to introduce evidence that could be mentioned at trial but that could not be present physically.

Examples might be the testimony of slaves obtained under torture or the offer to swear an oath (Harrison 1998, 147). Such challenges are mentioned frequently by the orators but probably were not accepted often. The infinitive is governed by κράτιστόν ἐστι. **λέγοντα:** If προκαλεῖσθαι had an expressed subject, it would be με. That implied pronoun also agrees with λέγοντα in the next clause.

5a6–a7   **περὶ πολλοῦ ἐποιούμην . . . εἰδέναι:** "I thought it was very important to know."

5a7   **ἐκεῖνος:** The pronoun refers to Meletus. **αὐτοσχεδιάζοντα:** "speaking offhandedly," that is, without having given a matter careful thought or having considered all necessary information (cf. *Euthphr.* 16a2; *Ap.* 20d1). Perhaps there is also a suggestion that by relying on his own resources, Socrates implicitly rejects Athenian *nomoi* as they are conventionally understood.

5a8   **καινοτομοῦντα:** See comm. on 3b6. Compare 16a4

5b1   **σοφὸν εἶναι τὰ τοιαῦτα:** "wise in respect to these things." Socrates continues to pretend that he regards Euthyphro as the latter confidently does. There is a double irony here. First, by making this description of Euthyphro subject to the approval of Meletus, Socrates draws attention to the fact that it is not necessarily accurate (cf. εἰ δὲ μή at 5b2). Second, by appealing to the authority of Meletus, who, to judge from his performance in the *Apology*, has neither interest in nor ability to judge questions about the gods, Socrates imagines a situation where questions of the highest order are to be determined by a pair of charlatans (Euthyphro and Meletus).

5b2   **ὀρθῶς νομίζειν καὶ ἐμὲ ἡγοῦ:** "believe that I also think correctly [i.e., like Euthyphro]." **εἰ δὲ μή:** The clause is parallel to καὶ εἰ μέν . . . ὁμολογεῖς at 5a9–b1.

5b3   **ἐκείνῳ τῷ διδασκάλῳ:** That Euthyphro is imagined to be Socrates' teacher continues the joke of 5a3-4. The idea that you should punish the teacher for the crimes of the student ironically parallels the idea of prosecuting Socrates for the crimes of men like Critias and Alcibiades, who were thought to be "students" of Socrates. For a rebuttal by Socrates, compare *Ap.* 33a5: ἐγὼ δὲ διδάσκαλος μὲν οὐδενὸς πώποτ' ἐγενόμην, "I was never anyone's teacher." The status of teachers in Plato is equivocal. Socrates recognizes that there can be teachers of technical things. He even claims the kithara player Connus as his own teacher (ὅς ἐμὲ διδάσκει, *Euthd.* 272c. See also X. *Smp.* 2.16, where Socrates solicits a Syracusan promoter for dancing lessons. Whether Socrates thinks that there are teachers for all subjects is less certain. The teachability of *arete*, "excellence," is a topic of discussion in *Protagoras* and *Meno.* λάχε δίκην: "file a charge." The legal idiom (+ dative of the person accused) omits reference to the actual filing of the charge and jumps to the end of the initial administrative process, when the schedule of cases to be heard would have been determined by lot (thus λάχε, < λαγχάνω, "obtain by lot").

5b4   πρεσβυτέρους διαφθείροντι: A joke parodying the indictment of Socrates for corrupting the youth.

5b5–b6   ἐμὲ μὲν διδάσκοντι ἐκεῖνον δὲ νουθετοῦντι τε καὶ κολάζοντι: "by teaching me [badly] and by correcting and punishing that man [Euthyphro's father]." Earlier in the dialogue (2b–c) Euthyphro had attempted to identify with Socrates on the ground that both were unappreciated by the city. Here, the father and Socrates are paired, linked by their age and their hypothetical treatment at the hands of Euthyphro. In this imagining of things, Euthyphro himself becomes very much like a rehabilitated Meletus, whom Socrates faults in the *Apology* for failing to take Socrates aside to teach and correct (διδάσκειν καὶ νουθετεῖν, 26a3–a4) and for not following the law that requires prosecution of someone needing punishment (κολάσεως) but not of someone who needs education (μαθήσεως, 26a7). The similar phrasing testifies clearly to a link between these two passages and, thus, to a structural resemblance between Euthyphro and Meletus.

5b6–b7   καὶ ἂν μὴ μοι πείθεται . . . σέ: After pretending to talk to Meletus, Socrates turns his attention back to Euthyphro.

5b7   αὐτὰ ταῦτα λέγειν: To render the infinitive and the punctuation as a question, supply ἆρ' οὖν μοι . . . κράτιστον (from 5a3), which is recalled by the repetition (from 5a5) of προκαλεῖσθαι.

5b8   ἃ προυκαλούμην αὐτόν: Socrates says that he shall inform the judges in court that his adversary has refused a challenge (that under the sound tutelage of Euthyphro, Socrates has changed his ways). Graves (1935, 63) aptly notes that this sentence illustrates how someone might make use of the *anaklesis* in court: "If the challenge was accepted the result settled the action. Here the challenge is that Meletus should give his opinion of Euthyphro's wisdom and abide thereby" (in either case, abandoning the present legal action against Socrates).

5b9–c1   εἰ ἄρα ἐμὲ ἐπιχειρήσειε . . . εὕροιμ᾽ ἄν . . . ἄν . . . ἐγένετο:
The huffy condition is mixed. The protasis and the first apodosis is a future-less-vivid construction ("If he should attempt . . . , I would discover . . ." The second apodosis (ἄν . . . ἐγένετο) is counterfactual: "there would have been more talk." At the beginning of the sentence, Euthyphro is merely insulted by the temerity of Meletus. By the end of the second apodosis, he treats the outcome of the entire imaginary affair as virtually certain. Some of the manuscripts have γένοιτο in place of ἐγένετο. Accepting this reading would simplify the construction by making the entire sentence future-less-vivid. However, γένοιτο seems like a banalization of the unexpected ἐγένετο.

5c1   σαθρός: "unsound," used of cracked pots. At *Grg.* 493e8, the word appears as a metaphor for unsound ideas; compare also *Tht.* 179d4.

5c2   περὶ ἐκείνου: "about him," that is, Meletus.

5c4   τοι: The particle expresses Socrates' ironic earnestness in the face of Meletus's bravado: "I really do want to become your student."

5c5–c6   ἄλλος πού τις καὶ ὁ Μέλητος οὗτος: "Meletus and everyone else, I suppose [που]." Socrates pretends to believe that Euthyphro's prowess has made accusers leery of attacking him. Denniston (1934, 491) describes που as expressing "assumed diffidence." It is very common in Plato, where this kind of pretense is an important part of Socrates' ironic style. The demonstrative with Meletus's name draws attention ironically to his lack of prominence (cf. 2b8).

5c6   οὐδὲ δοκεῖ ὁρᾶν: οὐ is taken closely with δοκεῖ (οὐ adhaerescent) and means "pretend not to." Compare, for example, Ar. *Eq.* 1146–47: οὐδὲ δοκῶν ὁρᾶν κλέπτοντας: "pretending not to see them as they steal." Burnet (1924, 110) sums up well Socrates' implication: "Euthyphro is ironically supposed to be so formidable that Meletus thinks it wiser to shut his eyes to his proceedings."

5c7   κατεῖδεν: Note κατιδών at 2c6. The repetition of the verb, with both instances referring to Meletus's prosecution of Socrates, effectively marks the end of the introductory scene and lays the groundwork for the ensuing discussion of τὸ ὅσιον.

5c8   οὖν: The particle is resumptive, bringing the conversation back to the issue of the holy and the unholy after the digression Socrates began at 5a3. **νυνδὴ:** "just now," in answer to Socrates' question at 4e4–e5: οὑτωσὶ ἀκριβῶς [a synonym for σαφῶς] οἴει ἐπίστασθαι περὶ τῶν θείων ὅπη ἔχει. This response picks up on Euthyphro's reply that he would not be worth much if he did not know accurately all things of this sort (4e–5a).

5d1   **περὶ φόνου καὶ περὶ τῶν ἄλλων:** The structure of the question is significant. περὶ φόνου refers clearly to the case of Euthyphro. By wanting to know what kind of things make up τὸ εὐσεβής (reverence) and τὸ ἀσεβής (irreverence), Socrates refers to the accusation against himself (for ἀσέβεια) as well. By adding the second term, περὶ τῶν ἄλλων (in regard to other things), he moves the discussion away from specific questions about which act is reverent or irreverent. This web of associations continues Socrates' conceit, according to which Euthyphro is a benevolent Meletus figure who will "teach and correct" Socrates rather than bring him into court (see comm. on 5b5). **ἢ οὐ ταὐτόν ἐστιν ἐν πάσῃ πράξει τὸ ὅσιον αὐτὸ αὑτῷ:** "Isn't the holy the same in every action [literally, itself (αὐτό) the same (ταὐτὸν) to itself (αὑτῷ)]?"

5d3   **αὐτὸ δὲ αὑτῷ ὅμοιον:** "itself similar to itself in every action" (supply ἐν πάσῃ πράξει). All individual examples of the holy and the unholy will have a basic sameness (also called μίαν τινὰ ἰδέαν) that allows us to call them "holy" and "unholy." If an action did not possess holiness (or unholiness), you could not call it holy (or unholy).

5d3–d5   **ἔχον μίαν τινὰ ἰδέαν:** "having a single form." Socrates asks for definitions—of τὸ εὐσεβές and its opposite—that can cover a range of specific examples (περὶ φόνου καὶ περὶ τῶν ἄλλων). Of interest is the appearance here of ἰδέα, which is also used to describe the abstract entities in Plato's Theory of Forms (see comm. on 6d11–e1). **κατὰ τὴν ἀνοσιότατα πᾶν ὅτιπερ ἂν μέλλῃ ἀνόσιον εἶναι:** "in regard to unholiness for everything that is going to be unholy." Unholiness may be expressed in many ways, but insofar as it is unholy (κατὰ τὴν ἀνοσιότητα), it will be the same (αὐτὸ δὲ αὑτῷ ὅμοιον, 5d3) for everything that is going to be (called) unholy (μέλλῃ ἀνόσιον εἶναι).

5d6   **Πάντως δήπου:** "Absolutely!" Despite the convolutedness of Socrates' generalization, Euthyphro supports it enthusiastically. He may have understood less than he lets on, however, as the ensuing discussion seems to indicate (see Burnet 1924, 112).

Two points have emerged from the discussion so far: (1) all holy actions are similar to the degree that they are holy, and (2) unholy actions are unholy because all of them possess unholiness. Consider the statements (1) it is holy to participate in public sacrifices, (2) it is holy to punish blood crimes, and (3) it is holy to follow the traditions of the city (τὰ νομιζόμενα). Each statement expresses the idea that a certain action is holy. Socrates assumes that a common element links the three statements (the holy) and that the element has the same meaning for each one (ἐν πάσῃ πράξει).

5d8–d10   τό . . . ὅσιόν ἐστιν . . . τῷ ἀδικοῦντι . . . ἐπεξιέναι: Euthyphro begins with an error characteristic of many Socratic interlocutors. Asked for a definition of the holy and the unholy in a form that will be true for each holy or unholy thing, he responds with an example of something he regards as holy (ὅπερ ἐγὼ νῦν ποιῶ). See Socrates' comment at 6d9–d10.

5d8   ὅπερ: "the very thing."

5d9   ἱερῶν κλοπάς: "temple robbery," also called ἱεροσυλία. It was punishable—at least in theory—with death. See Phillips 2013, 335–36.

5e2–e3   ὡς μέγα σοι ἐρῶ τεκμήριον: Indirect exclamation.

5e3   τοῦ νόμου ὅτι οὕτως ἔχει: Equivalent to ὅτι ὁ νόμος οὕτως ἔχει.

5e4   ὅτι ταῦτα ὀρθῶς ἂν εἴη οὕτω γιγνόμενα: "that these things would be done correctly in this way [i.e., the way that I am doing them by prosecuting my father]." μὴ ἐπιτρέπειν: "not to give in." The infinitive is dependent on οὕτως ἔχει. ὃ καὶ ἄλλοις . . . οὕτω γιγνόμενα is parenthetical.

5e5   μηδ᾽ ἂν ὁστισοῦν τυγχάνῃ ὤν: "no matter who he is" (literally, "not even if he happens to be whoever"). αὐτοὶ . . . οἱ ἄνθρωποι: The reference is to the family members of Euthyphro.

5e6   τυγχάνουσι νομίζοντες: "they happen to think"; that is, "it happens that they [already] think." They do not realize, Euthyphro thinks, that their present beliefs about the gods are inconsistent with their disapproval of him. τὸν Δία τῶν θεῶν ἄριστον καὶ δικαιότατον: Euthyphro assumes that the deeds of Zeus justify the same behavior among humans. That idea is mocked as an example of the new sophistical education in Aristophanes' *Clouds* (1081–83), where Zeus's serial adultery is used to justify the same behavior for humans. See also *Nu.* 1048–52, where bathing in warm water is defended by appealing to the warmth of "Heraklean baths" (Ἡράκλεα λουτρά, 1051; i.e., "hot springs"), created originally by Athena for Herakles' bathing. See Dover 1968, 224–25. Euthyphro here finds a model for his behavior in Zeus's willingness to punish his father Cronus.

6a2   πατέρα δῆσαι: The mythology of Cronus is complex. For the sources, see Gantz 1993, 44–48. The idea of binding (although absent in Hesiod) seems to be a persistent shocking thread. A. *Eum.* 641—αὐτὸς δ᾽ ἔδησε πατέρα πρεσβύτην Κρόνον, "He himself bound his old father, Cronus"—implies that Zeus has less care for the principle of honoring fathers (the murdered Agamemnon) than Apollo lets on. At *Euthphr.* 8b2—οὐδὲν θαυμαστὸν εἰ τοῦτο δρῶν τῷ μὲν Διὶ προσφιλὲς ποιεῖς, "It is not at all remarkable if in doing this, you do [a thing] that is dear to Zeus"—Socrates suggests ironically that Zeus will appreciate Euthyphro's attempt to punish his own father, as an emulation of Zeus. See also *Nu.* 905–6, where Unjust Speech's denial of the link between Zeus and justice is based specifically on Zeus's treatment of Cronus. τοὺς υἱεῖς: In Hesiod's version of the story, both sexes are swallowed indifferently. Athenagoras mentions an Orphic version, according to which only the males are swallowed (τοὺς ἄρσενας, *Pro Christ.* 20). For Orphic cosmogonies as emblematic of the sort of divine knowledge Euthyphro has in mind, see West 1966, 14. κατέπινεν: "swallowed." The same verb appears at Hesiod, *Th.* 459. To avoid potential usurpation of his power, Cronus swallowed his children as they emerged from Rhea's womb (*Th.* 459–62). οὐκ ἐν δίκῃ: Euthyphro used the same phrase at 4b9. His decision to prosecute his father has not been popular, and he will have had to defend his actions a number of times. His use of ἐν δίκῃ here makes it look like this myth was already in his thoughts at 4b9. κἀκεῖνόν: = καὶ ἐκεῖνόν. The indirect statement continues from ὁμολογοῦσι (6a1): "he also." Cronus had castrated his father, Uranus, who had imprisoned his newborn children in their mother, the earth (Γαίας ἐν κευθμῶνι, *Th.* 158). πατέρα: The object of ἐκτεμεῖν. Euthyphro's description of the castration is euphemistic. In the *Republic* Socrates refers to such stories about the gods as "lies" and refuses to let them be part of the new city (377d–378b).

6a3   δι᾽ ἕτερα τοιαῦτα: Like Cronus, Uranus had imprisoned his children to avoid the possibility of a rival for power.

6a4   ἀδικοῦντι: "for doing wrong." Euthyphro resents the attitude of his family members, who are angry at him and refuse to admit that his behavior is no different from Zeus's. In so thinking, Euthyphro shows an astounding indifference not only to the tradition of filial piety but to the shame associated with its violation. Although Socrates does not take up the issue of filial obedience here, he broaches the topic in the *Republic*, where (in language redolent of *Euthyphro*) he says that a young man should not punish his father when he does wrong (ἀδικοῦντα πατέρα κολάζων, 378b).

6a5   αὐτοὶ αὑτοῖς τὰ ἐναντία λέγουσι: "they contradict themselves."
Euthyphro reasonably assumes that if we decide to invoke principles in
one context, we should apply them consistently in others as well. This care
for avoiding self-contradiction is a common Socratic theme (cf., e.g., *Ap.*
27a3; *Prt.* 340b3; *Grg.* 482c3). Socrates differs from Euthyphro, however, in
encouraging his interlocutors to join him in a search for the principles on
which they all can agree, while Euthyphro takes his principles as already
embedded in the stories about the gods.

6a7   Ἆρά γε . . . τοῦτ᾽ ἐστιν οὗ ἕνεκα: "Is this why . . . ?"

6a8   γραφὴν φεύγω: "I am [currently] a defendant." Socrates tacitly rejects
Euthyphro's assumption at 3b5 that his current legal troubles arose from his
belief in the *daimonion*. That they arise from expressing doubt about the
Hesiodic (or Orphic) succession myth is unlikelier still (Burnet 1924, 114).
Ethical criticism of the traditional accounts is present already in Xenophanes,
fr. 11 D.-K. See also Isoc. 11.38–39. τὰ τοιαῦτα: "such things." Socrates refers
to stories like Zeus's violent overthrow of his father (see comm. on 6a2).

6a9   δυσχερῶς πως ἀποδέχομαι: "I have some difficulty accepting [it]."
δυσχερῶς ἀποδέχομαι may have some flavor of legal or rhetorical language
(Antiphon, *Tetr.* 2.2.4–5).

6a9–a10   φήσει τίς με ἐξαμαρτάνειν: In alluding to the prosecution of
Meletus (and others like him), Socrates picks up on Euthyphro's declaration
that one must prosecute anyone who does wrong (ἐξαμαρτάνοντι, 5d10),
regardless of status. In describing himself as someone who also will be
accused of wrongdoing, Socrates reinforces the parallel between himself and
Euthyphro's father. For Euthyphro and Meletus as doubles, see comm. on 5d1.

6a10   ταῦτα: Subject of συνδοκεῖ.

6b1   καὶ ἡμῖν: "for me also." The plural pronoun refers to Socrates alone;
so do φήσομεν and ὁμολογοῦμεν (6b2). Socrates has expressed reluctance
to trust in the old violent stories about the gods, but in the face of his own
admitted ignorance and of Euthyphro's claimed expertise about divine
matters, Socrates claims that he has no choice but to yield (συγχωρεῖν).

6b2-b3   αὐτοί . . . μηδὲν εἰδέναι: The phrase restates the principle of
Socratic ignorance, as Socrates expresses it in the *Apology* (e.g., 23b2–b4).

6b4   Φιλίου: Supply Διός. Zeus Philios is frequently invoked at banquets and represents the spirit of amity that is expected to prevail there (Burkert 1985, 107). Plato has Socrates appeal to Euthyphro in the spirit of friendship, which carries with it the obligation to speak frankly. Compare *Phd.* 234e2, where Phaedrus appeals to Zeus Philios to ask for Socrates' real opinion about the speech of Lysias, and *Grg.* 500b7 and 519e3, where Socrates urges on Callicles by appealing to the friendliness that Callicles expressed previously. See also Dodds 1990, 318. σὺ ὡς ἀληθῶς ἡγῇ ταῦτα οὕτως γεγονέναι: "do you really think these things happened this way?"

6b6   ἃ οἱ πολλοὶ οὐκ ἴσασιν: Euthyphro enjoys his special status as someone with privileged insight. Early in the conversation he complains about the envy of the ignorant members of the *ecclesia*, who fail to appreciate his mantic gifts (3c), and he has a distinct sense of his own superiority (4e9). If Socrates is referring to the same Euthyphro in *Cratylus* as in this dialogue, Euthyphro will have had a reputation for his knowledge of divine names (396d). For more on the character of Euthyphro, see comm. on 1.

6b7   τῷ ὄντι: "really." The article plus the participle is used here as an adverb.

6b9–c1   οἷα λέγεται τε ὑπὸ τῶν ποιητῶν, καὶ ὑπὸ τῶν ἀγαθῶν γραφέων τά τε ἄλλα ἱερὰ ἡμῖν καταπεποίκιλται: "the kinds of things said by the poets, and in addition [τὰ ἄλλα], our temples are adorned by the good painters." For another critical look at traditional mythology, see *Republic* 378d. The construction changes midway through this phrase, as the relative clause (οἷα) is abandoned and as a new main clause begins. Despite the change in construction, the two ὑπό phrases (expressing agency) and their verbs are in chiastic arrangement.

6c2   τοῖς μεγάλοις Παναθηναίοις: The Panathenaea was an important civic festival dedicated to Athena and celebrated annually. Its festivities included presenting Athena with a robe (πέπλος) woven by aristocratic Athenian girls. The Great Panathenaea, with additional events and contests, was celebrated every fourth year. For that event professional weavers may have woven a more elaborate robe depicting a variety of scenes, such as the Titanomachy (E. *Hec.* 466–74; *IT* 222–24) and the Gigantomachy. See Rhodes 1993, 568–69, on *Ath.* 48.3, discussing the design (παραδείγματα) of the peplos.

6c3   ποικιλμάτων: "embroidery." For the technology of the weaving, see

Barber 1992. ἀνάγεται: "is led up." The procession of the *peplos* began at the Pompeion and traveled along the Panathenaic Way before ascending to the Parthenon some 150 meters above.

6c5 Μὴ μόνον γε: "yes, not only." As Graves (1881, 67) notes, μή for οὐ here is under the influence of the deliberative subjunctive φῶμεν from the previous line. ἄρτι: compare θαυμασιώτερα at 6b5.

6c7 σύ . . . ἐκπλαγήσῃ: < ἐκπλήττω): "you will be amazed." Note the hyperbaton; Euthyphro postpones the verb for maximum dramatic effect.

6c8 εἰς αὖθις: "later." Socrates begins to bring Euthyphro back to the question at hand. See also 15e3, where Euthyphro repeats the phrase, not to keep the discussion on track, but to break it off entirely. These two senses of the expression are well represented in Plato. At *Euthd.* 275a4, *Grg.* 447c3, and *Prt.* 347b3, the offer to hear a sustained presentation of a topic, an *epideixis* or a *logos*, is deferred until "later." In the *Cratylus* (440e3) and the *Protagoras* (361e5), the phrase marks a transition to the end of a dialogue, as the result of a real or feigned need to attend to other matters.

6c9 πειρῶ: Imperative < πειράομαι: "try."

6d2 τὸ ὅσιον ὅτι ποτ᾽ εἴη: "what the holy is." The optative appears in a general relative clause in secondary sequence after the aorist participle, here equivalent to a secondary tense.

6d3 ὃ σὺ νῦν ποιεῖς: At 5d8, Euthyphro gave this as an example of τὸ ὅσιον, without articulating or defending what, precisely, made his action holy. Socrates is looking not for examples of the holy but for the trait or idea that is present in all holy things and allows us to call them that. Compare 6d-e.

6d6–d7 ἀλλὰ γάρ . . . ὅσια: "But really, Euthyphro, you say that many other things are also holy."

6d10 τῶν πολλῶν ὁσίων: Partitive genitive.

6d11-e1 εἶδος/ἰδέα: "shape, form." The two terms are related etymologically and do not seem to be distinguished here. They build on Socrates' formulation of the problem at 5d1–d2, where he referred to the essential idea that linked all instances of the holy (ταὐτὸν . . . ἐν πάσῃ πράξει). To put Socrates' present question in these terms, one could say, for example, that all things in the world that we call holy are holy to the degree that they share in the form of the Holy. The present terminology forms the basis for the Platonic Theory of Forms, according to which abstract entities like Goodness, Bigness, and Beauty allow us to make sense of the material world, although it is not at all clear from *Euthyphro* that Socrates sees the abstractions as having a separate existence. For a discussion of the Forms and other key Platonic doctrines, see Kraut 2017.

6e4 **δίδαξον:** The verb takes a double accusative.

6e5–e7 **ἵνα . . . φῶ:** The sentence is challenging to render because of the multiple subordinate clauses and two participial phrases that separate ἵνα from φῶ: "so that by paying attention [ἀποβλέπων] to that [ἰδέα] and using it as a standard, I may call holy whatever of the things that you or another do that are of that sort [i.e., whatever you or another does that is consistent with the παράδειγμα of the holy]." Such a template for the holy would allow Socrates to evaluate every act for its holiness and so presumably avoid further accusations of *asebeia*. The antecedent of ὧν has been ellipsed, while the relative itself has been attracted into the case of what that antecedent (e.g., τούτων) would have been.

6e6 **παραδείγματι:** "using it [αὐτῇ (τῇ ἰδέᾳ)] as a standard." The argument is that identifying "the holy itself" enables its use as a standard for determining which other things are—or are not—holy.

6e8 **καί:** "also," that is, "in addition to what I have already done." Euthyphro is willing to comply with Socrates' request, although he does not view it as requiring anything substantially different from what he provided with his first answer.

6e11 **τοῖς θεοῖς προσφιλές:** Euthyphro's second attempt to identify τὸ ὅσιον is to say that it is pleasing to the gods.

7a2 **Παγκάλως:** The adverb stands by itself as an exclamation of approval, referring to the whole of Euthyphro's answer, as ἀπεκρίνω shows. **ἐζήτουν:** "I wanted," followed by an accusative subject and an infinitive.

7a3 **ἀληθῶς:** Supply ἀπεκρίνω again in this clause.

7a4 **δῆλον ὅτι:** "clearly." The idiom appears frequently in Plato. ὅτι has no force as a conjunction (Smyth 1956, 2585). Compare *Prt.* 328e4, where it is collocated with the future of ἐπεκδιδάσκειν.

7a6 πάνυ μὲν οὖν: "Of course!" πάνυ strengthens an affirmation already strong.

7a7–a8 τό . . . θεοφιλὲς τε καὶ ὁ θεοφιλὴς ἄνθρωπος ὅσιος: The adjective describes both nouns but takes its gender from the second element only.

7a9 ἐστίν: The subject is τὸ ὅσιον. Both ταὐτόν and τὸ ἐναντιώτατον are predicates.

7a10 οὐχ οὕτως; "right?" In Euthyphro's response that follows, οὕτω gives an affirmative answer to οὕτως.

7b1 Δοκῶ: "I think so."

7b2 Οὐκοῦν: The word introduces a question expecting a "yes" answer. στασιάζουσιν: The word can refer to quarrels in a general sense but is used most commonly to describe political dispute (*stasis*) in which one faction rises up, or "takes a stand," against another. *Stasis* as discord is not usually associated with the gods. The members of the chorus of Aristophanes' *Knights* imagine that the goddess Nike fights (στασιάζει) by their side in a contest between rival choruses (590). More typically, however, the idea refers to discord at the polis level. Thus, Socrates' question suggests that he is evaluating divine behavior in human terms. In doing so, he tacitly contradicts Euthyphro, whose inclination is to evaluate human moral questions by appealing to divine codes of behavior, as in the case of Zeus binding Cronus (6a1). Disputes between gods are well represented in the mythological tradition. At the beginning of Euripides' *Hippolytus* (5–6, 21), Aphrodite implies that Hippolytus's excessive devotion to chastity in his service to Artemis is a form of ἀσεβεῖα. See also the mock theomachy at *Il.* 21.377–501.

7b5 Εἴρηται γάρ: "Yes, it was stated."

7b6 ἡ περὶ τίνων διαφορά: διαφορά picks up on διαφέρονται from 7b3 and anticipates διαφεροίμεθα in 7b7: "disagreement about what things?"

7b7 σκοπῶμεν: Hortatory subjunctive. To get the kind of answer he wants (ἡ περὶ τίνων διαφορά;) about the arguments that the gods have, Socrates draws parallels from other areas of life. If my friends and I dispute how the bill at a restaurant has been calculated, we are arguing about less or more. If my child is denied a ride on a roller coaster because the ticket taker does not think she is tall enough, we can argue about greater and lesser height.

If the airline representative will not accept my suitcase because of weight restrictions, our dispute is about heavier and lighter. In each of these cases, we do not get angry rightly or permanently because there are objective measures to solve each dispute.

7b8   ὁπότερα πλείω: "which [of two groups of] things is more [numerous]." πλείω is the contracted form of πλέονα. **ἡ περὶ τούτων διαφορὰ ἐχθροὺς ἂν ἡμᾶς ποιοῖ καὶ ὀργίζεσθαι ἀλλήλους:** "would disagreement about these things make us hostile and angry with each other?"

7b10   ἐπὶ λογισμὸν ἐλθόντες: "by counting." ἀπαλλαγεῖμεν: aorist passive optative < ἀπαλλάσσω: "we would be reconciled."

7c3   περὶ τοῦ μείζονας καὶ ἐλάττονος: "about greater or lesser [length]."

7c4   ἐπὶ τὸ μετρεῖν ἐλθόντες: "by measuring."

7c7   ἐπὶ ... τὸ ἱστάναι ἐλθόντες: "by weighing." For the sense of ἱστάναι, see LSJ, s.v. ἵστημι, A.IV.
     Three areas of dispute have been identified: number, length, and weight. For all three areas, the dispute can be resolved quickly by appealing to an objective standard. Socrates next moves to disagreements that are less easy to settle.

7c10-c11   Περὶ τίνος δὲ δὴ διενεχθέντες καὶ ἐπὶ τίνα κρίσιν οὐ δυνάμενοι ἀφικέσθαι: The two participial phrases take the place of two protases for the apodosis that follows (ἐχθροί γε ἂν ἀλλήλοις εἶμεν καὶ ὀργιζοίμεθα;). **διενεχθέντες:** < διαφέρω: "those who quarrel." κρίσιν, "decision," is a part of Socrates' formulation of the question under the influence of διακριθεῖμεν (7c8).

7c12   ἴσως οὐ πρόχειρόν σοί: "Perhaps you don't have anything at hand." The expression is impersonal. We must imagine that Socrates' question has produced an awkward silence. He now steps in to answer for Euthyphro by suggesting that justice, beauty, and goodness are the kind of things that provoke hard-to-resolve disputes.

7d2-d3   ἆρα οὐ ταῦτά ἐστιν: "Aren't these the things?"

7d4   αὐτῶν: As for ὧν the antecedent of αὐτῶν is ταῦτα (7d3).

7d5   ὅταν γιγνώμεθα: Supply ἐχθροὶ ἀλλήλοις from the previous clause. Differences of opinion do not necessarily lead to enmity. When they do, it is because of disputes regarding just and unjust, noble and shameful, and good and bad.

7d9   Τί δὲ οἱ θεοί; "What about the gods?" οὐκ: Take with δἰ αὐτὰ ταῦτα διαφέροιντ᾿ ἄν; εἴπερ τι διαφέρονται: "if they differ in any way." Socrates frequently hesitates to attribute human quarrels to the gods. See also 8d9, 8e7. In any case, Apollo implies such behavior is inappropriate at *Il.* 21.462–67, when he declines to fight with Poseidon for the sake of βροτῶν . . . δειλῶν, the gods need not develop lasting hatreds because of their differences.

7e1   ἄρα: "then." ἄρα draws an inference from πολλὴ ἀνάγκη. κατὰ τὸν σὸν λόγον: According to Euthyphro, the gods argue about the same things mortals do. Thus, Zeus's binding of Cronus (6a) must occur because they disagree about what things are just, holy, noble, and so on.

7e3   ἐστασίαζον: See comm. on 7b2. In using the vocabulary of *stasis* to describe the behavior of the gods, Socrates suggests (and Euthyphro affirms) that the actions of the gods can be understood in the same terms as the actions of humans (see also 8a1). Understanding human and divine behavior as equivalent paves the way for showing that τὸ ὅσιον cannot be defined simply as that which the gods collectively love. If the gods also quarrel over questions of what is good, just, or holy—as the mythological tradition assures us that they do—they must, like us, have different ideas of what constitutes the good, the just, and the holy. Thus, what is "loved by the gods" will be not a single thing but a group of things that may well be incompatible with each other.

7e4   ἦ γάρ: "right?"

7e7   ταῦτα καὶ φιλοῦσιν: "they also love these things [i.e., things that are beautiful, good, and just]."

7e10–8a1   ταὐτὰ δέ γε, ὡς σὺ φής, οἱ μὲν δίκαια ἡγοῦνται, οἱ δὲ ἄδικα: "So, some gods, as you say, think that [these] same things are just, and others that they are unjust." ταὐτά: = τὰ αὐτά. δέ γε: Picks up the thread of Socrates' previous question (Denniston 1934, 154).

8a4   ἄρα: "apparently." The word often signals Socrates' ironic distance by treating as surprising what he seems to have suspected all along.

8a6   Ἔοικεν: "It looks like it." Euthyphro's reply is unenthusiastic, as he begins to realize that his argument is slipping away. κινδινεύει at 8a9 is a similar reply.

8a8   τούτῳ τῷ λόγῳ: Socrates is careful to show that although he is committed to examining Euthyphro's argument to test its validity, he does not necessarily accept its premises. See also κατὰ τὸν σὸν λόγον at 7e2, with its emphatic possessive adjective, and ὡς σὺ φῄς at 7e10; both function in the same way.

8a10–a11   οὐ γὰρ τοῦτο γε ἠρώτων: The argument has shown that the essential quality of the holy cannot be that it is pleasing to the gods, as Euthyphro understands them, since the gods' habit of disagreeing with each other would end up making the same action holy to one god but unholy to another. Socrates criticizes Euthyphro for telling him what is both holy and unholy, when the philosopher's original request was to identify the holy itself. The form of the rebuke is ironic, since it pretends to be ignorant of the fact that Euthyphro thought he was answering Socrates' question correctly.

8a12   ὃ δ᾽ ἂν θεοφιλὲς ᾖ καὶ θεομισές ἐστιν: "Whatever is pleasing to the gods is also hated."

8b2–b3   Διὶ προσφιλὲς . . . τῷ Οὐράνῳ ἐχθρόν: By emulating the behavior of Zeus, Euthyphro is dear to Zeus (who did the same thing to his father) but hateful to Uranus, who was castrated by his son Cronus (Hesiod, *Th.* 180–82).

8b4   Ἡφαίστῳ φίλον τῇ δὲ Ἥρᾳ ἐχθρόν: The strained relations between Hera and her son are well known. At *Il.* 18.395–97, Hephaestus describes having been thrown out of Olympus by his mother to hide his lameness. See also *H. Ap.* 316–20. In a related story, Hephaestus created a chair that he sent as a gift to his mother. Fitted with invisible chains, the chair made it impossible for her to stand. Pausanias (1.20.3) tells the story, but it was known in Plato's time (see *Alc.*, fr. 349 *P.LF.*). For the myth as a whole, see Gantz 1993, 74–78. The incident is also mentioned at *Rep.* 378d, in the context of a catalog of mythological stories that are not worthy of emulation and are thus unsuitable for the guardians of the new city.

8b6   κατὰ τὰ αὐτά: "in the same way," that is, by making each individual dear to some and hateful to others.

8b7–9c1   Euthyphro objects that although disputes between them may be common, the gods do not disagree on the fundamental principle that evildoers should be punished. Socrates does not disagree with Euthyphro but points to the fact that agreement in principle does not mean agreement about specific instances of injustice. In a trial, both sides accept this principle but disagree about whether it applies to the actions of the accused.

8b7   περί γε τούτου: "about this, anyway." τοῦτο refers to the content of the ὡς clause that follows. Euthyphro believes that he has a valid point to make against Socrates' argument, at least as it concerns Euthyphro's own situation as a man punishing his father. He points out that although the gods may argue, none of them think that criminals should get off without punishment. His objection misses the point, however. The gods accept the principle of punishment in general but dispute the application of it. Zeus and Cronus would agree that punishing wrongdoers is good, but each of those gods would deny that they are wrongdoers themselves.

8b9   ἐκεῖνον: Subject of διδόναι.

8b10–c2   τινὸς . . . ἀμφισβητοῦντος ὡς τὸν ἀδικῶς ἀποκτείναντα . . . δίκην διδόναι: "someone arguing that it is not necessary for a man who has killed unjustly or is doing anything else unjustly to be punished [δίκην διδόναι]."

8c3   μὲν οὖν: Here, as often, μὲν οὖν is strengthened with the repetition of a word from the preceding speech (ἀμφισβητοῦντος, ἀμφισβητοῦντες). Euthyphro substitutes a more emphatic version of Socrates' statement that he regards as having been insufficiently emphatic (Denniston 1934, 475): "Have I ever heard them arguing? On the contrary, they never stop arguing."

8c5   φεύγοντες: The defendant is often referred to as ὁ φεύγων. In that construction, as here, the present participle is conative: "attempting to flee."

8c8   οὐ . . . φασί: "deny." See similar usage at 8d10. The question, now clarified, is not "Do the gods argue?" but "About what do they argue?"

8c10   Οὐκ ἄρα πᾶν γε: "not everything, then." ἄρα . . . γε sharpens Socrates' correction of Euthyphro's assertion that defendants stop at nothing to secure acquittal: πάντα ποιοῦσι καὶ λέγουσι (8c5). τολμῶσι: Humans do not dare to make this claim, because it contradicts traditional assumptions about the gods as guarantors of justice. Compare 8d11–e1.

8d1   δοτέον: Verbal adjective < δίδωμι. Supply εἶναι: "they don't dispute [ἀμφισβητεῖν] . . . that a penalty must be paid."

8d6   τὸ τίς ἐστιν ὁ ἀδικῶν, καὶ τί δρῶν καὶ πότε: "who committed the crime, what he did, and when?" τό turns the three questions into a collective noun, as though a familiar refrain: "your basic who, what, and when." The phrase is without parallel, however. Compare ἔστιν δὲ τί τὸ ἔγκλημα καὶ τίνος ἡ δίκη; at 4a9. All the questions nevertheless point to issues that might be enough to secure the acquittal of a defendant without challenging the legitimacy of the court.

8d9   εἴπερ στασιάζουσι: "to the degree that they do quarrel."

8e1   τολμᾷ: Compare 8c11. Socrates assumes that the same constraints on moral behavior observable among humans are present among the gods. But if the gods establish such standards for humans, whose strictures constrain their "daring"? In thus setting up the problem, Socrates hints at important issues that the dialogue will take up: what makes the holy "holy," and what is the relationship of the gods to it? Is the holy "holy" because the gods love it? Or do they love it because they recognize its holiness? Put differently, do the gods determine what is holy on their own, or does that determination come from somewhere beyond the gods, and is holiness simply *appreciated* by them? If the gods determine what is holy, why do they seem to argue about it so much? If the gods simply appreciate holiness, its source lies above the gods, in which case it is unclear what the gods do or why we ought to worship them.

8e3–e4   τό γε κεφάλαιον: "for the most part, anyway." Euthyphro has no substantive objection to make here, but, as Burnet says (1924, 122), "Euthyphro's sense of superiority is not easily disturbed, and he will not assent without a reservation."

8e5   Ἀλλ᾽ ἕκαστόν γε: Socrates insists that the structure of disagreements between men and between the gods is not true "for the most part" but true for each action.

8e7   πράξεώς τινος πέρι: Note the anastrophe of the preposition, as well as the lack of a connective to link the prepositional phrase and what follows with the sentence before the colon (explanatory asyndeton).

9a1–a8:   This complex sentence has multiple levels of subordination. Socrates asks for evidence (τεκμήριον) of two things: (1) that all the gods think that the worker was killed unjustly and (2) that it is right for Euthyphro to prosecute his father. Lines 9a1–a7 summarize the facts of the case as they concern the *pelates*, who is referred to specifically at the beginning (ἐκεῖνον ἀδικῶς τεθνάναι) and at the end (καὶ ὑπὲρ τοῦ τοιούτου). Introduced by ὅς ἄν . . . φθάσῃ, the facts are presented in a general relative clause, to which a πρίν clause is subordinated. πυθέσθαι, the main verb of the πρίν clause, introduces an indirect question (τί χρὴ ποιεῖν). Note the explanatory asyndeton that characterizes the entire description.

9a2   τί σοι τεκμήριον ἐστιν; "what is your evidence?" **πάντες θεοί:** The addition of πάντες is necessary if it is true that the gods disagree on the most basic issues of justice, a point Euthyphro has conceded. To maintain that he is acting in a way that is holy, then, he must offer some evidence (τεκμήριον) that there is a divine consensus in his favor.

9a3   **τεθνάναι:** For ἀποθνήσκω as the passive of ἀποκτείνω, see comm. on 4b4.

9a5–a6   **φθάσῃ τελευτήσας διὰ τὰ δεσμὰ πρίν τὸν συνδήσαντα . . . πυθέσθαι:** "died first on account of his bonds before the one who tied him up . . . learned . . ." Translate φθάσῃ (anticipates) as an adverb (i.e., "first") and τελευτήσας as if it were the main verb. φθάσῃ is subjunctive in a general relative clause (introduced by ὅς ἄν in 9a3). For the details of the case, see 4c–d. On the use of an accusative subject plus an infinitive in πρίν clauses, see Smyth 1956, 2453.

9a6   **περὶ αὐτοῦ:** "concerning him"; that is, what ritual or legal procedures should be followed in regard to the murder of the slave by the *pelates*.

9a7   **ὑπὲρ τοῦ τοιούτου:** That is, on behalf of a man who was already a criminal himself.

9a8   **ἐπισκήπτεσθαι:** "denounce." The verb usually refers to a counterclaim to an assertion that a case was illegal or invalid (διαμαρτυρία). Cases already entered into would stop at the point of the διαμαρτυρία until the legality of the charge had been adjudicated. In Euthyphro's case such a process could have been used by his family to deny that he had standing to bring a charge against his father, since the *pelates* was not a family member. See comm. on 4d7; Phillips 2013, 221.

9b3 ἐγκωμιάζων: The supplemental participle is standard with the middle of παύω: "I will not stop praising." ἐπὶ σοφίᾳ: Socrates' references to the wisdom of Euthyphro are an important motif in the dialogue (see, e.g., 3d6, 4b1, 12a5) and remind us of the ironic distance between Euthyphro's uncritical self-assessment and Socrates' recognition that Euthyphro has never pushed himself (cf. τρυφᾷς at 12a5) to acquire anything but a semblance of wisdom. For the ambivalent status of wisdom in *Euthyphro*, as well as in Plato generally, see comm. on 2c5.

9b6 ἐπεί: "since." The word is apparently elliptical here. Understand something like "since I could explain it to you [if there were enough time]."

9b7 δικαστῶν: Genitive of comparison. δυσμαθέστερος: "slow to learn." Socrates pretends that his own inability to learn, rather than the incoherence of Euthyphro's explanations, prevents progress in understanding. According to the worldview provided by the concept of "Socratic ignorance" (see comm. on 5a3–b8), the "wise man" (Euthyphro) is a fool, while slow learners like Socrates are actually much wiser.

9b8 δῆλον ὅτι: "clearly." The expression is completely adverbial; ὅτι does not function as a conjunction. ἄδικα: Supply ταῦτα, referring to the alleged crimes of Euthyphro's father.

9b10 ἐάνπερ ἀκούωσί γέ μου λέγοντος: "to the degree that they listen to me when I am speaking." Euthyphro's uncertainty that the clarity of his explanation will be noticed suggests the anxiety that his experience with the jurors may be similar to his reception before the *ecclesia* (cf. 3c).

9c1 ἐάνπερ εὖ δοκῇς λέγειν: Socrates' words anticipate those of Euthyphro at 9b10. They put the blame for failure back on Euthyphro, however, and tacitly contradict Euthyphro's complaints about not getting a fair hearing. Socrates' words here apply both to Euthyphro's previous appearances before the *ecclesia* and to the upcoming trial. On multiple occasions in the *Apology* (e.g., 17a6–b1, 19e5–a2), Socrates refers to the difficulty of making himself heard before an audience predisposed not to listen to him.

9c1–d6 τόδε δέ σου ἐνενόησα . . . καὶ τοῦ ἀνοσίου: After the digression on whether people accept the principle of punishing someone who has acted unjustly (see comm. on 8b7–9c1), Socrates returns to the idea, established earlier, that the existence of disputes among the gods means that the same things can be regarded as both holy and unholy.

9c2   σοῦ . . . λέγοντος: Genitive absolute: "while you were talking."
The present participle indicates time contemporaneous with the main verb
(ἐνενόησα).

9c4–c6   τί μᾶλλον ἐγὼ μεμάθηκα παρ' Εὐθύφρονος τί ποτ' ἐστὶν τὸ
ὅσιον τε καὶ τὸ ἀνόσιον; "what more do I understand from Euthyphro with
respect to what the holy and the unholy are?" Even if Euthyphro can show
that all of the gods hate someone who has killed unjustly, that conclusion
presumes a definition of the holy, which is still unknown.

9c6   τὸ ἔργον: The reference is to the actions of Euthyphro's father that
resulted in the death of the *pelates*.

9c7   οὐ τούτῳ ἐφάνη ἄρτι ὡρισμένα τὸ ὅσιον καὶ μή: "the holy and
the unholy did not turn out just now to be determined by this." Although
Euthyphro had wanted to equate τὸ ὅσιον with what is loved by the gods,
he later admitted that the same things are both holy and unholy (8a7–a8).
Thus, as Socrates says here, knowing that something is loved by the gods is
not sufficient to define it as holy. As Woodruff (2016) writes, "The essence of
reverence [i.e., τὸ ὅσιον] cannot be conferred on reverent actions by the gods'
approval of them; their approval, rather, must follow on their partaking of the
essential nature of reverence. So actions are made reverent not by pleasing a
god, but by satisfying the definition of reverence." Socrates offers Euthyphro
an opportunity to revise his definition to limit the holy and the unholy to
what all the gods love and hate, respectively, allowing for the possibility that
there are actions that will not fulfill either condition.

9d1   ἡγείσθων . . . μισούντων: Third person imperatives: "let [all the
gods] think . . . and . . . hate."

9d1–d6   ἀλλ' ἄρα τοῦτο . . . καὶ τοῦ ἀνοσίου: "But this thing that we are
now revising in the argument, that what all the gods hate is unholy, and what
they all love is holy, and what some love and some hate is either both (holy
and unholy) or neither—do you want it to be defined in this way concerning
the holy and the unholy?"

9d2   τοῦτο: The pronoun is explained by the ὡς clause (9d2–d5).

9d7   γάρ: The particle is slightly elliptical. It presumes a "yes" answer on
which the explanatory γάρ expands.

9d8–d9   Οὐδὲν ἐμέ γε . . . ἀλλὰ σὺ δὴ τὸ σὸν σκόπει, εἰ τοῦτο
ὑποθέμενος οὕτω ῥᾷστά με διδάξεις: "Nothing prevents me, anyway, but
you—consider your situation [τὸ σόν], whether by assuming this, you will
so easily teach me what you promised." Socrates' reply begins with a witty
literalization of a common idiom to criticize Euthyphro's tendency to speak
thoughtlessly (see also comm. on 14e9). τί κωλύει (with the answer οὐδέν
either expressed directly or implied) and the similarly used οὐδὲν κωλύει
appear forty-seven times in Plato to assert that there is nothing to prevent
the speakers from considering the question at hand in a particular way. The
opposite idea, that κωλύει could have a subject other than οὐδέν (i.e., that
nothing prevents Socrates but that something could prevent someone else),
appears only in this passage and at *Chrm.* 163a6. Here, as often, Plato avoids
easy parallelism: instead of "nothing prevents me, but something prevents
you," the construction shifts emphatically.

9d8   σὺ δή: Denniston (1934, 207–8) suggests that this combination is
particularly "ironical, contemptuous, or scornful" and that each of those
senses is rendered into English by intonation. All are possible here, but
irony is the most likely. Socrates often expresses himself in such a way, to
call attention to the limitations of the partner in the conversation without
sacrificing the intellectual issues at hand. Compare his remarks to Callicles
at *Grg.* 487e8 and those of the Eleatic stranger at *Sph.* 232e6. Euthyphro
complacently accepts Socrates' proposed revision that the holy is what all the
gods love. However, Socrates cajoles him to test the new observation.

9e4   ἐπισκοπῶμεν: Deliberative subjunctive, like ἐῶμεν (< ἐάω, "accept")
in the next line.

9e6   ἐὰν μόνον φῇ τίς τι ἔχειν οὕτω: "if someone simply [μόνον] says that
something is like this."

9e8   μέντοι: "however."

10a1   εἰσόμεθα: Future < οἶδα. While the general sense of the following
passage is fairly clear, translating it is complicated by the occasional obscurity
of the demonstrative pronouns and by uncertainty about the referent of each
definite article plus neuter pronoun—for example, whether τὸ θεοφιλές is to
be understood as the idea of being loved by the gods or as a particular thing
loved.

10a2–a3   ἆρα τὸ ὅσιον ὅτι ὅσιόν ἐστιν φιλεῖται ὑπὸ τῶν θεῶν, ἢ ὅτι
φιλεῖται ὅσιόν ἐστιν; "is the holy loved by the gods because it is holy [ὅτι
ὅσιόν ἐστιν], or is it holy because it is loved by the gods?" The question is
initially bewildering, although it has been lurking in the conversation that
precedes it. Euthyphro thinks that the holy can be defined as whatever is
"loved by all the gods." The basic question is whether the opinions of the gods
are relevant to the question of the holy. This is expressed as a dilemma. On the
one hand, if the gods love something because it is holy, they do not determine
the holiness in that thing: its holiness exists whether the gods love it or not.
On the other hand, if things are only holy because the gods love them, the
idea of the holy is incoherent, since it has already been established that the
gods do not love and hate the same things.

Socrates has doubts that the holy can be defined just as something that all
the gods love; this point motivates his warning to Euthyphro at 9d8–d10. In
developing his critique, Socrates distinguishes between characteristics that
reveal something essential about an object and those that are incidental to
the essence of the object. For example, we can speak of a pink house, but we
could just as easily have a house that is green, since a house of any color can
provide shelter and whatever else being at a house involves. Is being loved by
the gods similar to having a pink house? To answer that question, Socrates
develops an analogy based on the distinction between active and passive voice
in verbs. For example, there is seeing (ὁρῶν)—someone or something seeing
something—and a thing seen (ὁρώμενον). Yet it makes no sense at all to
talk about a "seen" book, for example, unless there is someone or something
present to look at it. Moreover, the book continues to exist whether someone
sees it or not. Thus, the attribute "seen" cannot be part of the definition of
"book," since that attribute only expresses characteristics that are inessential.
If the attribute "loved by the gods" (θεοφιλές) is comparable to the attribute
"seen," it expresses not an essential characteristic of the holy but an inessential
one. Such a result cannot produce a definition of the holy, as Euthyphro
thought it would.

10a5–a6   λέγομέν τι φερόμενον: "We refer to something 'carried.'"

10a8   ἕτερα ἀλλήλων: "different from each other." ἀλλήλων is a genitive
of comparison: carrying is different from being carried. καὶ ᾗ ἕτερα: "and how
they are different."

10b1–b2   Λέγε δή μοι, πότερον τὸ φερόμενον διότι φέρεται φερόμενόν
ἐστιν, ἢ δι ' ἄλλο τι; "Tell me, is something carried <called> 'carried' because
it is being carried, or for some other reason?" Socrates repeats this formula

for the other verbs mentioned. Although the distinction between active and passive is fundamental to the way Greek is taught nowadays, I am not aware of discussion of the idea in any literary sources prior to Plato. Socrates' presentation of the idea therefore presents problems to us as readers, since it does not draw on a preexisting way of articulating this distinction. In this sense, our difficulties mirror those of Plato's original audience. Instead of working to master concepts that have long intellectual histories, we are witnesses to thought in the making. It brings frustration but also excitement.

10b4   **διότι ἄγεται:** "because it is being led."

10c2–c3   **εἴ τι γίγνεται . . . γιγνόμενόν ἐστι:** "if something happens or has something happen to it [literally, experiences something], it is happening not because it is [i.e., because we call it] a thing 'happening' but because it is happening [i.e., taking place]."

10c7–c8   **Οὐκοῦν καὶ τὸ φιλούμενον ἢ γιγνόμενόν τί ἐστιν ἢ πάσχον τι ὑπό του;** "Therefore, isn't the thing that is loved also either becoming something or experiencing something at the hands of someone/something?" Mostly throughout this technical discussion, a participle with the article (e.g., τὸ φιλούμενον) serves as the subject, while an adjective without the article comprises the predicate. Compare also 10d12: οὐκ ἄρα τὸ θεοφιλὲς ὅσιόν ἐστιν, ὦ Εὐθύφρων οὐδὲ τὸ ὅσιον θεοφιλές, "So, apparently, something loved by the gods is not holy, Euthyphro, nor is the holy loved by the gods."

10c10–c12   **οὐχ ὅτι φιλούμενόν ἐστιν . . . φιλούμενον:** Before returning explicitly to τὸ ὅσιον, Socrates draws a connection between things that are loved and the earlier examples of passives that are passive (things seen, carried, etc.) because someone or something acts upon them (by seeing them, carrying them, etc.): "something loved is loved [φιλεῖται] by those who love it not because it is a 'loved thing' [i.e., something loved independently of any actual lover], but it is a 'loved thing' because it 'is loved' [i.e., because someone actively loves it]."

10c11   **ὑπὸ ὧν:** Short for ὑπὸ τούτων ὑπὸ ὧν.

10d2   **ἄλλο τι:** "Is it anything other than that . . . ?" The full form of the phrase is ἄλλο τι ἤ. See, for example, *Phd.* 64c4: ἆρα μὴ ἄλλο τι ἢ τὴν τῆς ψυχῆς ἀπὸ τοῦ σώματος ἀπαλλαγήν; "Can [death] be anything other than the separation of the soul from the body?" See also *Ap.* 24c9.

10d4   Socrates returns to the question of what makes the holy "holy."
From the perspective of most human beings, who are content simply to
follow the traditions that have been handed down by their ancestors (τὰ
νομιζόμενα), it is enough to know generally what the gods require (according
to the revised definition) and to attempt to comply. Socrates shifts the
discussion here, however, to suggest that the gods love what they love because
it is holy (ὅτι ὅσιόν ἐστιν). Making a comparison to a "carried thing," which
can be described as "carried" only when someone is carrying it, Socrates
asks whether what all the gods love (the holy) is loved because it is holy (and
would continue to be holy whether recognized by the gods or not).

10d5   Οὔκ, ἀλλὰ διὰ τοῦτο: Οὔκ responds to δι᾽ ἄλλο τι. τοῦτο picks
up ὅτι ὅσιον εστιν: "No, not for another reason, but because of this [because
it is holy]." Euthyphro's affirmative answer here (διὰ τοῦτο) will doom his
amended argument that the holy is defined by what all the gods love: if the
gods love the holy because it is holy, holiness possesses an essential quality
that is not affected by love (or anything else).

10d12   Οὐκ ἄρα τὸ θεοφιλὲς ὅσιόν ἐστιν: "Apparently [ἄρα], the thing
loved by the gods is not holy." It would have been more precise for him to
say οὐδὲ τὸ ὅσιον τὸ θεοφιλές, "Nor are the holy and the god-loved the
same" (Burnet 1924, 129). Something is already holy or unholy before the
preferences of the gods enter the picture. Euthyphro does not grasp Socrates'
surprising conclusion. It will require a review of the previous argument to
tease it out for him (10e2–11b5).

10e6-e7   Τὸ δέ γε θεοφιλὲς ὅτι φιλεῖται ὑπὸ θεῶν, αὐτῷ τούτῳ τῷ
φιλεῖσθαι θεοφιλὲς εἶναι: "Because it is loved by the gods, the god-loved
thing, by that very act of being loved, is god-loved."

10e10–11a3   Ἀλλ᾽ εἴ γε ταὐτὸν ἦν, ὦ φίλε Εὐθύφρων, τὸ θεοφιλὲς καὶ
τὸ ὅσιον, εἰ μὲν διὰ τὸ ὅσιον εἶναι ἐφιλεῖτο τὸ ὅσιον, καὶ διὰ τὸ θεοφιλὲς
εἶναι ἐφιλεῖτο ἂν τὸ θεοφιλές, εἰ δὲ διὰ τὸ φιλεῖσθαι ὑπὸ θεῶν τὸ θεοφιλὲς
θεοφιλὲς ἦν καὶ τὸ ὅσιον ἂν διὰ τὸ φιλεῖσθαι ὅσιον ἦν: Socrates summarizes
the argument to show how τὸ θεοφιλές is not the same as the holy by pointing
to a contradiction in the idea as it has been discussed: "If the god-loved and
the holy were the same, and if the holy were loved because of its holiness, and
if the god-loved were loved because of its being god-loved, the holy also [καί]
would be holy on account of being loved [by the gods]."

11a3   νῦν δέ: "as it is."

11a4   ἔχετον: Present active indicative third-person dual. ἑτέρω: Nominative dual neuter (so also ὄντε).

11a4–a5   τὸ μὲν (θεοφιλές) . . . τὸ δὲ (ὅσιον): Socrates offers another formula for distinguishing accidental (unnecessary) qualities from essential ones. τὸ θεοφιλές is a thing loved because—and only because—it happens to be loved (οἷον φιλεῖσθαι). Nothing about that status is connected to something essential. τὸ ὅσιον is a thing loved simply by virtue of being what it is.

11a7   ἐρωτώμενος: "when you are asked." The present participle perhaps suggests repetition, as in "each time you are asked."

11a8   οὐσίαν: "being." Socrates distinguishes here between οὐσία, which indicates the essence of a thing (without which it necessarily would be something else), and πάθος (condition), which refers to a thing's qualities that do not affect its οὐσία. Euthyphro continually fails to make that distinction. Whereas Socrates asks for a definition (*ousia*) of the holy, Euthyphro is only able to supply a *pathos* of it (e.g., that it is loved by the gods). For a similar error, see *Grg.* 448d–e. οὐ βούλεσθαι δηλῶσαι: Socrates ironically portrays Euthyphro's inability to answer his questions as unwillingness. Compare Socrates' similar attempts to cast Euthyphro as his teacher (see comm. on 3b3).

11a9   ὅτι πέπονθε: This short explanatory clause glosses πάθος by pointing to the shared derivation from πάσχω. Socrates evidently imagines the term to be unfamiliar to Euthyphro. See Adam 1890, 86.

11b1   ὅτι δὲ ὄν: "what it is." The subject of the participle is τὸ ὅσιον and appeals to the shared etymology of ὄν and οὐσία. See Adam, 1890, 86. εἰ οὖν σοι φίλον: This phrase is a polite request, in a sense, but also plays on the long discussion of θεοφιλές and φιλεῖσθαι.

11b3   εἴτε φιλεῖται ὑπὸ θεῶν εἴτε ὁτιδὴ πάσχει: "whether it is loved by the gods or has some other [nonessential] characteristic [literally, whatever it experiences]." οὐ γὰρ περὶ τούτου διοισόμεθα: < περιφέρω: "we will not argue about this." Both alternatives refer to the πάθοι of τὸ ὅσιον; that is, they do not express the essence of the thing (τί ποτε ὄν) and are therefore not worth argument.

11b6–b7   οὐκ ἔχω ἔγωγε ὅπως σοι εἴπω ὃ νοῶ: Euthyphro is reduced to the kind of *aporia* experienced by many Socratic interlocutors. Frequently described in colorful terms, the experience points to what an extraordinary impression Socrates made on Plato. In *Meno* (80c6), talking with Socrates is compared to the numbing effect of the electric ray (νάρκη, for which see the exhaustive note at Bluck 1961, 268–69). The practice of describing humans with animal comparisons is familiar from the fables of Aesop and seems to have been popular. See, for instance, Ar. *V.* 1308–10, with the note at Biles and Olson 2016, 464–65; see also X. *Smp.* 5.7. Here, Euthyphro's complaint that his arguments will not stay in the same place reminds Socrates of the story that the statues of Daedalus were so lifelike that they had to be chained down so they would not walk away (cf. *Men.* 97d, with the note at Bluck 1961, 408–11). This comparison leads Euthyphro, in turn, to charge that Socrates is a modern Daedalus whose words produce similar results (11d1). ἀεί: "each time."

11b8   ἱδρυσώμεθα: < ἱδρύω, "cause to sit": "set up." The middle is used frequently to describe the erection of statues and the dedication of temples. The verb thus anticipates the references to sculpture that follow.

11b9–c1   Τοῦ ἡμετέρου προγόνου . . . Δαιδάλου: The reference is to Daedalus, the famous sculptor and inventor. See comm. on 11b6, where striking comparisons are used to describe the unique quality of undertaking a conversation with Socrates. Socrates mentions an ancestral connection with Daedalus at *Alcibiades I* 121a3, presumably on the basis of the tradition preserved by Diogenes Laertius (2.18), that Socrates' father, Sophroniscus, was a sculptor (and thus a metaphorical descendent of Daedalus) and passed the art to his son (at *Tht.* 148e–151d, however, Socrates claims to have inherited the skills of midwifery from his mother and to use them to help his associates give birth to philosophical ideas). There is no evidence that Socrates ever worked as a sculptor. The statues seen by Pausanias and thought to have been Socrates' work (Paus. 1.22.8) were probably the work of another.

11c1–c2   εἰ . . . ἔλεγον καὶ ἐτιθέμην . . . ἐπέσκωπτες: The point of the present contrafactual is that the meandering arguments are not those of Socrates at all but Euthyphro's. See 11c5: σαὶ γὰρ αἱ ὑποθέσεις. Socrates imagines that if the situation were reversed and if he were making Euthyphro's arguments, Euthyphro would make fun of him and connect his words with the deeds of Daedalus (ἐκείνου, 11c3). ἐτιθέμην picks up on Euthyphro's προθώμεθα (11b7). Where a compound verb needs to be repeated, Plato will often do so by using the uncompounded form. See, for example, *Rep.* 336e: εἰ γὰρ ἐξαμαρτάνομεν . . . ἄκοντες ἁμαρτάνομεν, "If we err, we err unwillingly."

11c3 τὰ ἐν τοῖς λόγοις ἔργα: "[my] verbal works of art." See X. *Mem.* 3.10.7 for statues as ἔργα. ἀποδιδράσκει: "run off." The arguments of Euthyphro, like the statues of Daedalus, are imagined to act like escaping slaves, with whom the verb ἀποδιδράσκω is often associated.

11c5–c6 ἄλλου . . . τινος . . . σκώμματος: "some other joke." Since, unlike Socrates, Euthyphro cannot claim that he's being true to his ancestry by making arguments that can't keep still, some other joke is needed to explain their behavior.

11c6–c7 καὶ αὐτῷ σοι δοκεῖ: "as it seems also to you" (see 11b6).

11c8 σχέδον τι: "pretty much." The phrase adds a degree of imprecision to a comment that otherwise might be perceived as overly specific.

11c9–c10 τὸ γὰρ περιιέναι αὐτοῖς τοῦτο: Articular infinitive: "this walking around of theirs." The phrase is coordinate with μὴ μένειν ἐν τῷ αὐτῷ, for which supply τό. περιιέναι continues the idea of περιέρχεται at 11b7.

11d1 ἀλλὰ σύ μοι δοκεῖς ὁ Δαίδαλος: "but it's you who seem to be the Daedalus." Euthyphro resists the idea that his arguments could be at fault. He protests, instead, that Socrates is the real Daedalus. By speaking in this way, Euthyphro temporarily drops his superior tone and adopts a kind of populist anti-intellectualism that treats careful distinctions and nuanced conclusions with distrust. In another sense, however, his comment suggests a metaphor for philosophy. Under the scrutiny of Socrates, previously unexamined beliefs come unmoored and walk off like a statue with working legs. On the troubling effects of Socratic questioning elsewhere in Plato, see comm. on 11b6. ἐμοῦ γε ἕνεκα: literally, "as for me, anyway," in the sense of "if things were left up to me" or "as far as my contribution goes." ἔμενεν ἄν: "they would stay put." The same verb was used at 11c6 and 11c10 to describe what the errant arguments of Euthyphro refuse to do (see also 11d5).

11d3 ἐκείνου τοῦ ἀνδρός: "than that man." Burnet (1924, 132) believes that a more grandiloquent effect is intended (i.e., "than my venerated ancestor"). See also Adam (1890, 89).

11d4 δεινότερος: "shrewder." For the pejorative sense of the term, see comm. on 3c8. τὴν τέχνην: "with respect to my skill." See Smyth 1956, 1600. τοσούτῳ, ὅσῳ: Translate only the second correlative: "to the degree that."

Forms of τοσοῦτος are ellipsed frequently in expressions like this. Compare, for example, 12a4; *Ap.* 39d2. **ὁ μέν:** Daedalus. **τὰ αὑτοῦ μόνα:** "only his own works."

11d6   **καὶ τὰ ἀλλότρια:** "those of other people as well." **τῆς τεχνῆς . . . κομψότατον:** "most refined [part] of my art." In Plato, forms of κομψός are often used ironically, as here, to suggest a kind of spurious refinement or elegance that would not really stand scrutiny. See, for example, *Cra.* 426a2, where appealing to ἐκδύσεις . . . μάλα κομψαί, "very refined excuses," is contrasted with offering an account of how things really are; see also *Hp. Ma.* 288b4. **σοφός:** Not "wise" but "clever." Given the importance attached to σοφία in the dialogues, however, it is difficult to avoid seeing more here. Of particular importance is the reluctant conclusion Socrates draws in the *Apology* (22e6–23c1) after his conversations with the politicians, the poets, and the craftsmen that his awareness of his own ignorance is itself the highest expression of human wisdom (*Ap.* 23a5–b4). See comm. on 2c5. This ignorance is on display in *Euthyphro* as well, where Socrates pretends to expect that Euthyphro is an expert teacher of holiness who will instruct him, who knows nothing. In this passage Socrates' "unwilling" cleverness/wisdom, like the reputation he gained after visiting the politicians, the poets, and the craftsmen, comes from his demonstrations that Euthyphro's pretensions to knowledge were unjustified and incoherent.

11e1   **πρὸς τῇ Δαιδάλου σοφίᾳ τὰ Ταντάλου χρήματα:** "the wealth of Tantalus together with the skill of Daedalus." The Phrygian king Tantalus, the father of Pelops and Niobe, was one of the great criminals punished in Hades (see Pi. *O.* 1). He was also famously wealthy, to judge from Socrates' use of the alliterative proverb τὰ Ταντάλου τάλαντα, "the talents of Tantalus" (see also Anacr. *PMGF* 355; Isoc. 5.144). Socrates would prefer arguments that stayed still (i.e., kept to the point and resulted in definite conclusions) over the combined resources of Daedalus and Tantalus.

11e2   **τούτων . . . ἅδην:** "enough of these things." **τρυφᾶν:** "live luxuriously"—perhaps equivalent here to something like "You are not accustomed to hard work." See comm. on 12a5.

11e3   **συμπροθυμήσομαι:** "I will eagerly join."

11e4   **μὴ προαποκάμῃς:** "don't tire out early [προ-]!" Socrates hints that Euthyphro's habit of living luxuriously (τρυφᾶν) may have left him out of shape. Socrates begins a new line of argument here with the suggestion that the holy is related to "the just."

11e5   δίκαιον εἶναι πᾶν τὸ ὅσιον: "all of the holy is just." Socrates begins to probe for places where holiness and justice do not line up.

11e7   Ἆρ᾽ οὖν καὶ πᾶν τὸ δίκαιον ὅσιον; "So, is all of the just holy? Or is all of the holy just but not all of the just holy, but part of it is just and the rest something else?" Take πᾶν together with τὸ δίκαιον (here and at 12a1). Forms of πᾶς in the predicative position refer to each instance of an individual or an idea, whereas forms in the attributive position refer to a collectivity. Thus, πάντες οἱ πολῖται means "all citizens" as individuals, but οἱ πάντες πολῖται refers to the citizen body as a whole. See Smyth 1956, 1174b.

11e7–12a2   ἆρ᾽ οὖν καὶ πᾶν τὸ δίκαιον . . . τι καὶ ἄλλο: Socrates suggests that the holy and the just are not identical and that the holy is a subset of the just. Thus, all holy things are just, but not all just things are holy. Contrast, for example, Sophocles' Antigone, who can imagine the just and the holy to be at odds. In thinking of herself as already having buried Polynices against the express decree of Creon, she refers to herself as "having stopped at nothing in the doing of holy things" (ὅσια πανουργήσασ᾽, *Ant.* 74).

12a4   Καὶ μὴν νεώτερός γε: "But you are younger" (and therefore should be quick to catch on). γε is determinative here, emphasizing νεώτερος: "this and only this" (Denniston 1934, 119–20). ὅσῳ: Parallel with ἔλαττον. Both are used adverbially: "younger [than I] by no less than you are wiser."

12a5   ὑπὸ πλούτου τῆς σοφίας: Socrates has already compared Euthyphro to Daedalus, who is known for his *sophia* (11e1). The mention of wealth points to the "talents of Tantalus," which Socrates also rejected. The abundance of Euthyphro's resources (as Socrates pretends to believe) has habituated him to an easier life (τρυφᾷς). See also 11e2: μοι δοκεῖς σὺ τρυφᾶν.

12a6   σύντεινε σαυτόν: "exert yourself" (in opposition to the languor implied by τρυφᾶν at 11e2). At *Phd.* 98d, the verb describes the contractions of νεῦρα (sinews) that allow the limbs to move.

12a7   τὸ ἐναντίον ἤ: Supply ὅ: "the opposite to that which . . ." ὁ ποιητὴς ἐποίησεν ὁ ποιήσας: The lines that follow are from the *Cypria*, the part of the Epic Cycle that narrated the story of the Trojan War from its earliest stirrings in the determination of Zeus to punish humans down to the events just prior to the beginning of the *Iliad*. There may be a larger thematic resonance with between *Cypria* and the *Euthyphro*. According to the scholiast on *Il.* 1.5 (fr. 1 Davies), Zeus did so because of mankind's great *asebeia*. The scholiast on *Il.*

1.5 attributes authorship of the poem to Stasinus. The alliterative vagueness of ὁ ποιητὴς ἐποίησεν ὁ ποιήσας suggests that its authorship is not known to Socrates, however. Aristotle is similarly non-committal on that front: ὁ τὰ Κύπρια ποιήσας (*Po.* 1459b30).

12a9–b1   Ζῆνα δὲ τὸν ἔρξαντα . . . ἔνθα καὶ αἰδώς: "He/she is unwilling to blame Zeus, who in acting, sowed all of this; for where there is fear, there is shame" (fr. 24 Davies). For additional comments on the fragment see Currie 2015, 281–305.

12a9   Ζῆνα: Accusative form of Ζεύς. Compare *Il.* 14.157, with the note at Janko 1994, 172.

12b1   ἵνα: "where." δέος . . . αἰδώς: The subject of the sentence apparently fears Zeus and thus refrains from criticizing him. This reticence to speak is understood as a species of shame. For the ability of an internalized αἰδώς to produce self-restraint for fear of losing honor, see Cairns 1993, 13, 372 n. 83.

12b2   εἴπω: Deliberative subjunctive.

12b4   οὐ δοκεῖ μοι εἶναι: "It does not seem to me to be [true]."

12b5–b6   νόσους καὶ πενίας καὶ ἄλλα πολλὰ τοιαῦτα: Take all of the accusatives as objects of the participle δεδίοτες. In Socrates' previous example, it turned out that while all holy things were just, not all just things were holy (12a). The same structure appears here with shame and fear: since we fear and avoid shame, we can say that all shameful things are objects of fear. The inverse, however, is not true, for we fear things (disease, poverty, etc.) that are not shameful. Thus, Socrates rejects the *Cypria*'s assertion (quoted at *Euthphr.* 12a9–b1) that shame and fear are always copresent.

12b9–b10   ἔστιν ὅστις: "is there anyone who. . . ?"

12b10–b11   αἰδούμενος . . . αἰσχυνόμενος . . . πεφόβηται . . . δέδοικεν: The pairs are largely synonymous. See Cairns 1993, 138–39; for the connection between *aidos* and *phobos*, 371–78.

12c1   δόξαν πονηρίας: Both *aidos* and *aischune* are social concepts in that they refer to how others would perceive it if one made certain claims about oneself or acted in a certain way.

12c2   Δέδοικε μὲν οὖν: "He certainly fears." The particle combination here signals Euthyphro's strong agreement with what Socrates has said. μὲν οὖν often represents a lively engagement with the speech of another person, from direct contradiction to strong assent. See Denniston 1934, 476–77.

12c5   ἐπὶ πλέον: Supply ἐστίν: "[is] more extensive." αἰδοῦς: Genitive of comparison.

12c6   μόριον γὰρ αἰδὼς δέους: Socrates now explicitly formulates the distinction he has been implying: fear and shame are related but not identical. Like species is related to genus in a biological taxonomy, so the less inclusive category here, shame, is a part of the more inclusive one, fear. For example, all tigers are members of the genus *Panthera*, but not all members of the genus *Panthera* are tigers; leopards, lions, and jaguars belong to that genus as well. In the same way, shame is a part of fear, although not all fears bring shame.

12c8   Ἕπῃ γάρ που νῦν γε: "You do follow me now, don't you? ἕπῃ continues the metaphor from 12a3 (ἕπομαι).

12c10   τὸ τοιοῦτον τοίνυν . . . λέγων: "meaning just this sort of thing." ἐκεῖ: "then." The temporal sense of the adverb is uncommon but not unprecedented. Compare Demosthenes 22.38.

12d2–d3   μόριον γὰρ τοῦ δικαίου τὸ ὅσιον: Socrates now explicitly subjects his earlier questions about the just and the holy to the approach he has developed based on the relationship between species and genus.

12d4   οὔκ: So accented when followed by a pause: "No."

12d5   τὸ μετὰ τοῦτο: "the next point."

12d6-d7   τὸ ποῖον μέρος ἂν εἴη τοῦ δικαίου τὸ ὅσιον: "the part of the just the holy would be." Socrates has already established that the holy is not identical to, and thus must be only a part of, justice, just as "odd" is part of numeration but not the whole thing.

12d7–d8   τι τῶν νυνδή: "one of the things [we were talking about] just now."

12d8-d9   ποῖον μέρος ἐστὶν ἀριθμοῦ τὸ ἄρτιον καὶ τίς ὢν τυγχάνει

οὗτος ὁ ἀριθμός: "what part of numeration 'even' is and what this number is."

12d9   ὅτι ὃς ἄν: "that [it is] whichever one . . ." **μὴ σκαληνός . . . ἀλλ᾽ ἰσοσκελής:** Both terms are taken from geometry. σκαληνός means "unequal" (< σκάλλω, "turn over" as with a hoe, thus probably "make uneven"). Such triangles have three unequal sides. ἰσοσκελής means "with equal legs," thus "even"—that is, capable of being bisected into two equal halves.

12e2   Μελήτῳ: For the idea that by instructing Socrates about the holy, Euthyphro will convince Meletus to withdraw his prosecution of Socrates, see comm. on 5a3–b8.

12e4   ἀδικεῖν: Earlier (at 2d–3a), Socrates had ironically pretended that Meletus was a kind of careful farmer who protected the young, the new shoots of the city, from corrupting forces like himself. Here he abandons this joke and portrays Meletus as someone actively wronging him.

12e5   μεμαθηκότας: The participle takes its temporal significance from λέγωμεν, which pretends to imagine a future time after Euthyphro has at last taught Socrates about the holy. It goes without saying that Socrates has no real expectation that Euthyphro can provide that lesson. **τά . . . εὐσεβῆ:** The expression is not to be distinguished from τὰ ὅσια here. By including it, however, Socrates explicitly links the present conversation with the charge of *asebeia* lodged by Meletus.

12e7–e9:   Euthyphro divides the just into two parts, one concerned with care (*therapeia*) of humans, the other with care of the gods. τὸ ὅσιον is equivalent to the latter. **τὸ περὶ τὴν τῶν θεῶν θεραπείαν:** "the one concerned with care of the gods." εὐσεβές and ὅσιον are both predicates. **θεραπεία:** The word has numerous senses, a fact that Socrates proceeds to explore.

12e8–e9   τὸ λοιπὸν . . . μέρος: "the remaining part."

13a2   ἥντινα ὀνομάζεις: "to which [*therapeia*] you refer." **οὐ γάρ που λέγεις γε, οἷάπερ καὶ αἱ περὶ τὰ ἄλλα θεραπεῖαί εἰσιν, τοιαύτην καὶ περὶ θεούς:** "Surely, you don't mean that the gods receive the kind of care that are also applied to other things?" The style of Socrates' remark appears to imitate the diffuseness of oral speech. In the next line, λέγομεν . . . φαμεν produces a stuttering effect.

13a4   οἷόν φαμεν: "for example, we say . . ."

13a4–a5 ἵππους οὐ πᾶς ἐπίσταται θεραπεύειν, ἀλλὰ ὁ ἱππικός: The superiority of expert opinion is asserted frequently in the dialogues. See, for example, *Ap.* 20b, where Socrates, in denying that he ever was anyone's teacher, recounts a conversation in which he asked an acquaintance for information about a real teacher, an ἐπιστάτης who is τῆς . . . ἀρετῆς τῆς ἀνθρωπίνης τε καὶ πολιτικῆς ἐπιστήμων, "knower of human and civic excellence"; compare also *Ap.* 25a–b.

13a5 ἱππικός: Less "horse trainer," in the sense of someone who performs a specific job, than a person with a particular knowledge and expertise. Adjectives in -ικός are popular in fifth-century texts and seem related to "sophistic" innovations in education. Aristophanes regularly mocks people who use them, especially to discuss fashionable topics like rhetoric (e.g., *Eq.* 1378–81). Nevertheless, the -ικός formulation is ubiquitous in Plato (and Xenophon), for whom it is important to emphasize that the ability to do a certain job is dependent on the type of knowledge (τέχναι) that allows such actions to be done intentionally. Compare Socrates' contention in *Gorgias* (463b4) that rhetoric is produced not by *techne* but by ἐμπειρία καὶ τριβή (experience and habit). Here in *Euthyphro*, θεραπεία plays the role occupied by *techne* in other dialogues. For the complex sociolinguistic history of adjectives ending in -ικός, see Willi 2003, 139–45.

13a7 θεραπεία: Translate twice: "Surely equine care is the care of horses."

13a10 ὁ κυνηγετικός: The pattern continues: knowledge about the care of hunting dogs is not available to everyone, just to the person who understands the principles. κυνηγετικός does not appear in fifth-century texts or inscriptions or in the work titled either κυνηγετικός or κυνηγετικά and attributed to Xenophon.

13a12 ἡ . . . κυνηγετική . . . θεραπεία: See comm. on 13a7.

13b4 Ἡ . . . ὁσιότης τε καὶ εὐσέβεια: Socrates omits arguing for the connection between this example and the foregoing one: *hosiotes* and *eusebeia* are types of *therapeia* and should be entrusted to experts in this type of knowledge. If the point is conceded, however, it is clear that just as the herdsman's occupation is the care and improvement of cattle, so that of the specialist in *hosiotes* is the care and improvement of the gods.

13b7 ταὐτὸν διαπράττεται: "accomplish the same thing."

13b8   **οἷον τοιόνδε:** "[I mean] something like the following." The lack
of precision is a conversational tactic intended to suggest Socrates' affability.
In fact, he asks for something quite precise. **ἐπ᾽ ἀγαθῷ τινι:** "with a view to
something good." **τοῦ θεραπευομένου:** Objective genitive with ὠφελίᾳ. See
also τοῦ θεραπευομένου at 13c2. The trap begins to close again. By having
acknowledged that *therapeia* is performed with a beneficial end in mind (ἐπ᾽
ἀγαθῷ τινι . . . καὶ ὠφελίᾳ), Euthyphro implies that *hosiotes* and *eusebeia*
benefit the gods, thereby making them better (13c7–c9).

13c6   **θεραπεία οὖσα θεῶν:** "inasmuch as it is care of the gods."

13c8–c9   **βελτίω τινὰ τῶν θεῶν ἀπεργάζῃ:** "make one of the gods better."

13c12   **πολλοῦ καὶ δέω:** "I am far from that, too."

13d3   **ὀρθῶς:** Attach the adverb to something like ἥγῃ, picking up on
ἡγούμενος from the previous line.

13d5   **τίς . . . θεῶν θεραπεία εἴη ἂν ἢ ὁσιότης;** "what [sort of] care of the
gods would holiness be?"

13d6–d7   **Ἥνπερ . . . οἱ δοῦλοι τοὺς δεσπότας θεραπεύουσιν:** "the very
kind that slaves give their masters." For humans as slaves to the gods, see *Phd.*
62b: ἕν τῶν κτημάτων τοῖς θεοῖς εἶναι.

13d8   **ὑπηρετική:** "serving." The adjective is derived from ὑπηρετής,
"rower," but refers more generally to anyone who performs a service. Although
this serving is not strictly synonymous with slavery, the two ideas are paired
at Ar. *V.* 602: δουλείαν καὶ ὑπηρεσίαν, "slavery and servitude." The gender of
ὑπηρητική suggests that θεραπεῖα should be understood, although the idea
of τέχνη is not far away. For the similarity between this argument, based on
various types of θεραπεῖα (and their objects), and arguments based on various
notions of *techne*, see comm. on 13a5. Socrates returns to the idea of ὁσιότης
as ὑπηρεσία at 14d6.

13d10–d11   **ἡ ἰατροῖς ὑπηρετικὴ εἰς τίνος ἔργου ἀπεργασίαν τυγχάνει
οὖσα ὑπηρετική:** "for the production of what product is the art that serves
doctors useful?" ἀπεργησίαν, cognate also with ἔργου, picks up on ἀπεργάζῃ
(13c9). The highly wrought sentence, which establishes a new template for
Euthyphro's latest attempt to define τὰ ὅσια, helps to link this part of the
discussion with what has gone before.

13d11–d12   εἰς ὑγιείας: Supply ἀπεργησίαν from 13d10.

13e1   τί δέ: "What about. . . ?"

13e10   Socrates observes that the medical art serves doctors and results
in health, that the art of shipbuilding serves the shipbuilder to produce boats,
and that the art of carpentry helps a carpenter to produce houses. If τὰ ὅσια/
ὁσιότης is a service in the same way, he argues, service to the gods should
also have a product. Noting that any product of the gods would certainly
be something altogether beautiful (πάγκαλον, 13e12) but that many things
could be so described, he asks what sort of altogether beautiful thing the gods
produce (14a9).

14a1   πολλὰ καὶ καλά: Euthyphro does not answer Socrates' question.
He simply repackages πάγκαλον in such a way as to highlight the many
instances of the πάγκαλον ἔργον. Thus, Euthyphro has not made consistent
progress from earlier in the dialogue, when he thought he could define τὰ
ὅσια by listing one or more of its characteristics (see comm. on 6d3). As a
result, Socrates again must teach Euthyphro the proper way of answering the
question in terms of universal propositions.

14a2   καὶ γὰρ οἱ στρατηγοί: "So do generals." τὸ κεφάλαιον: See comm.
on 8e3.

14a11   πρότερον: The reference is to 9b4.

14b1   μαθεῖν: Dependent on πλείονος ἔργου (genitive of value).

14b2   κεχαρισμένα: < χαίρω: "things rejoiced at." Just as was the case with
the understanding of the holy as "loved by the gods" (θεοφιλές), so the idea
of supplying the gods with τὰ κεχαρισμένα will fail if it is unable to answer
follow-up questions like "Why do the gods rejoice at these things?" and "What
do these things offer that the gods do not already have?"

14b5   ἰδίους οἴκους καὶ τὰ κοινὰ τῶν πόλεων: Under Euthyphro's new
formulation, τὰ ὅσια is understood as the correct application of prayer and
sacrifice. In making this claim, Euthyphro drastically restricts the application
of τὰ ὅσια to a narrow field of ritual activity dominated, presumably, by
priests. Certainly, any Greek would have agreed with him that the domain
of τὰ ὅσια is the preservation of individual households and cities, but by
restricting it as he does, Euthyphro appears to leave little to the actions

of individuals, beyond those engaging in religious activities, both within
the home and publically. This new definition diverges significantly from
the concerns of the dialogue: (1) that Euthyphro is practicing τὰ ὅσια by
prosecuting his father and (2) that Socrates' newly learned understanding of
τὰ ὅσια will allow him to persuade Meletus that the philosopher will no longer
engage in *asebeia*. Neither of these specific situations can be understood
as primarily connected to prayer and sacrifice. They are the activities of
the expert/priest. What compels Euthyphro to prosecute his father is not
Euthyphro's role as a *mantis* but his view that he is doing as everyone ought.

14b7   ἦ: "truly." **πολύ . . . διὰ βραχυτέρων:** Supply λόγων: "with many
fewer words." The prepositional phrase should be taken with the apodosis
that follows (εἶπες ἄν . . .). Socrates is not an enemy of verbosity for its
own sake. However, he resists attempts by his interlocutors to take control
of conversations by directing them away from points he views as crucial.
In this sense, the content of *makrologia*, as he terms it, is not bad; it is just
irrelevant. For Socrates as the opponent of *makrologia*, see *Prt.* 334d; see also
Grg. 461e2–e3, where Socrates reflects ironically that Polus, having come to
Athens, the place of the greatest freedom of speech in all of Greece (οὐ τῆς
Ἑλλάδος πλείστη ἐστὶν ἐξουσία τοῦ λέγειν), will not be allowed to answer at
whatever length he wishes (ὁπόσα ἂν βούλωμαι).

14c1   **οὐ πρόθυμός με εἶ διδάξαι:** Again, Euthyphro's inability to
comprehend τὰ ὅσια is presented, ironically, as unwillingness (cf. 3d6, with
comm.). For the imagined attitude of Euthyphro here (οὐ πρόθυμος), see
11b4: ἀλλ᾽ εἶπε προθύμως τί ἐστιν τό τε ὅσιον καὶ τὸ ἀνόσιον.

14b8–c1   **καὶ γὰρ νῦν ἐπειδὴ ἐπ᾽ αὐτῷ ἦσθα, ἀπετράπου:** "When you
were on the verge [ἐπ᾽ αὐτῷ] just now, you turned away." Socrates alludes
vaguely to a lost opportunity at some recent point in the dialogue. Perhaps
he refers to 13e12, when Socrates had asked Euthyphro to provide the
πάγκαλον ἔργον that service to the gods allows humans to accomplish.
Another approach would be to take ἐπ᾽ αὐτῷ as referring to13c8–c9, where
Socrates asks for confirmation of his statement that "when you do a holy
thing, you make one of the gods better." Had Euthyphro not been so shocked,
it would have been possible to return to the shocking stories about the gods
on which Euthyphro's self-confidence is based and which Socrates appears
reluctant to accept. Such an approach, if followed to the end, would have
led to the conclusion that the gods' behavior must be directed toward an
idea of the Good, which, in turn, would reveal τὸ ὅσιον to be a *therapeia*
that acknowledges the goodness of the gods, makes it visible to humans,

and creates a human behavior standard based on the desire to become as much like the gods as possible. For a similar idea, see *Tht.* 176b, where escape from the human realm is called ὁμοίωσις θεῷ κατὰ τὸ δυνατόν (the greatest possible similarity to the gods) and said to be δίκαιον καὶ ὅσιον μετὰ φρονήσεως (just and holy with intelligence). Euthyphro's recognition and taking of such an opportunity might have satisfied Socrates, but it seems unlikely that this approach would have reassured those who resented Socrates' antinomianism, since the approach strikes at the heart of τὰ νομιζόμενα by abandoning the tradition of individualistic and independent Olympians, in favor of gods constrained at every step of the way by the need to be as good as possible.

14c3 ἐμεμαθήκη: The pluperfect appears in place of the aorist and emphasizes the ongoing effect of the verb. The resulting clause thus gives a mild expression to Socrates' (perhaps feigned) impatience with Euthyphro: "I would have learned [and so already would know]." For the pluperfect in conditions, see Smyth 1956, 2006a, 2310d.

14c4 τὸν ἐρωτῶντα τῷ ἐρωτωμένῳ ἀκολουθεῖν: "the questioner must follow the one being questioned." The text is uncertain here. The reading of the manuscripts that comprise the β family (for the key to the sigla, see Duke et al. 1995, 2) is τὸν ἐρῶντα . . . τῷ ἐρώμενος: "The lover must follow the beloved." That is also the reading of the corrector (T²) of Codex Venetus App. Cl. 4.1 (T), thought by some to have been Arethas, the bishop of Cappadocia and original owner of Bodleian MS E. D. Clarke 39 (B), the earliest (late ninth-century) representative of the β family. The problem is complicated further by the fact that, as Adam (1890, 101) saw, the same confusion of ἐρωτᾶν and ἐρᾶν exists elsewhere in Plato at *Rep.* 437c and *Erastae* 132d.

Nor can the correct reading be determined by appealing to the greater intelligibility of one variant over the other, as each yields a text that is both readable and contextually plausible. If, on the one hand, we accept the text of Duke, et al., Socrates alludes to one of the governing conditions of the Platonic dialogue: as questioner, Socrates must follow where the various answers of Euthyphro (τῷ ἐρωτωμένῳ) lead, since Socrates' practice is not to give lectures but to assist others in developing their own insight. This way of seeking wisdom is not economical, since, as Socrates complains here, the questioner cannot hold the questioned one to the subject but must follow him wherever he (metaphorically) goes. Thus, τὸν ἐρωτῶντα τῷ ἐρωτωμένῳ ἀκολουθεῖν makes perfect sense in a Platonic dialogue, especially this one, in which the interlocutor of Socrates is rather self-satisfied and not particularly gifted as a thinker.

If, on the other hand, we accept the β reading, Socrates structures the rhetorical situation of himself and Euthyphro according to the norms of pederastic courtship, within which the adult male lover (τὸν ἐρῶντα, elsewhere described as an *erastes*) pursues a reluctant *eromenos* and so must follow wherever his object of desire leads. As is clear from the speech of "Lysias" in *Phaedrus* (230e–34c), pederastic courtship could be rationalized as pedagogical in nature, a view facilitating a philosophical application of the metaphor here, with Socrates as the lover and Euthyphro as the beloved who must be pursued to become wiser. The speech of Alcibiades at *Smp.* 215a–227b gives both a version and an inversion of how this might work. For Socrates as an idiosyncratic *erastes* of Alcibiades, see *Alc. I* 103a; *Prt.* 309a. For the *erastes* and *eromenos* relationship in Athenian law, see Cohen 1991.

Both readings invoke important themes in the Platonic dialogues. On the surface of things, the latter reading seems more interesting. It also has the advantage of connecting *Euthyphro* with other dialogues that thematize the relationship between philosophy and eros. In support of this connection, Burnet (1924, 139) connected Socrates' use of τρυφᾷς (11e2, 12a5) with *Men.* 76b, where the participle τρυφῶντες is used to describe the caprice of an *eromenos* pursued by an *erastes*. However, the most interesting reading is not *ipso facto* the correct one. The interest of the Platonic dialogues in the relationship between eros and philosophy could just as easily have inspired a copyist to alter an original τὸν ἐρωτῶντα τῷ ἐρωτωμένῳ to an "improved" τὸν ἐρῶντα τῷ ἐρώμενος.

14c8   οὐκοῦν τὸ θύειν δωρεῖσθαί ἐστι τοῖς θεοῖς; "Isn't the act of sacrifice [τό ... θύειν] [the same as] making offerings to the gods?" δορεῖσθαι is the predicate, operating as a verbal noun.

14c9   αἰτεῖν: Supply ἐστί from the previous line.

14d1   Ἐπιστήμη ... αἰτήσεως καὶ δόσεως θεοῖς ὁσιότης: Euthyphro's final attempt at a definition is that holiness is the knowledge of asking from and giving to the gods. Here, ὁσιότης is a calculus of knowing how to ask for things from the gods and knowing what and how to sacrifice to them. From the perspective of religions that emphasize the importance of nonrational factors like faith, redemption, and damnation, Euthyphro's proposal seems extremely businesslike. This *do ut des* mentality would have seemed far less odd to an Athenian, however.

14d3   συνῆκας: < συνίημι: "understand." Euthyphro persists in taking seriously Socrates' frequent assertions that Euthyphro has wisdom that

Socrates does not. Euthyphro therefore congratulates Socrates on finally understanding the point Euthyphro is trying to make.

14d5 οὐ χαμαὶ πεσεῖται: "it will not fall to the ground." Pindar uses a similar construction to describe the envious man whose neglected thought falls to the ground (*N.* 4.41, χαμαὶ πετοῖσαν; see also *O.* 9.12, χαμαιπετέων, of words that, like badly aimed arrows, could fail to hit their mark).

14d9–d10 Ἄρ᾽ οὖν οὐ τό γε ὀρθῶς αἰτεῖν ἂν εἴη ὧν δεόμεθα παρ᾽ ἐκείνων, ταῦτα αὐτοὺς αἰτεῖν: "Wouldn't asking correctly [τό . . . ὀρθῶς αἰτεῖν] be asking them [αὐτούς] for these things that we need from them?"

14d11 Ἀλλὰ τί; "What else?" (= "Of course").

14e2 δεόμενοι: The participle is supplementary with τυγχάνουσιν. παρ᾽ ἡμῶν: At 13c10, Euthyphro recoiled at the thought that his *therapeia* made the gods better (see also 15a7), but the concept of "need" is difficult for his position, in that it already implies a defective condition that could be improved. At any rate, things that I need are inevitably dear to me, a point that Socrates will raise at 15b to describe the feelings of the gods about τιμή and γέρα they receive from humans. For Euthyphro, τὸ ὅσιον is essentially providing the gods with τὸ θεοφιλές, a definition that has already been rejected (10d).

14e2 οὐ γὰρ που τεχνικόν γ᾽ ἂν εἴη δωροφορεῖν διδόντα: The expression is impersonal: "It certainly would not be an expression of the art [τεχνικόν] for the giver to give gifts." δωροφορεῖν suggests bribery, as at Ar. *V.* 675; Socrates may be suggesting that Euthyphro's idea of *hosiotes* is rather seedy. This idea is continued at 14e6, when Socrates brands it an ἐμπορευτική . . . τεχνή, "business art."

14e8 εἰ οὕτως ἥδιόν σοι ὀνομάζειν: "if you want to call it that." Euthyphro is reluctant to see *hosiotes* as a moneymaking venture, although jokes about greedy priests are a standby in Old Comedy. His petulant tone reflects irritation, perhaps at Socrates' triumphant ἄρα in 14e6.

14e9 οὐδὲν ἥδιον ἔμοιγε: For Socrates' willingness to call out Euthyphro for his careless replies and lack of interest in their philosophical implications, see comm. on 9d8–d10.

14e11–15a5: Socrates holds out the possibility that the gods' emporic skills are not very advanced; the gods obviously give out many things but may receive nothing of value in return.

15b1   **κεχαρισμένον:** The idea that τὸ ὅσιον produces χάρις (15a11) allows Socrates to conclude that it is also κεχαρισμένον. Something that "gratifies" the gods might be imagined as dear to them (θεοφιλές), as Euthyphro quickly reaffirms (15b5), forgetting that the explanation of τὸ ὅσιον as τὸ θεοφιλές has already been proposed and rejected (10d).

15b8   **φαίνωνται μὴ μένοντες:** "they clearly don't stay in the same place." For φαίνομαι with the participle, see Smyth 1956, 2143. **αἰτιάσῃ . . . βαδίζοντας αὐτοὺς ποιεῖν:** "you accuse me of making them [the arguments] walk." ποιεῖν is causative here, as is ποιῶν at 15b10.

15b9   **τὸν Δαίδαλον:** Predicative with με: "you accuse me of being Daedalus." Socrates reprises the argument about who is to blame for the incoherence of Euthyphro's ideas (see comm. on 11d1). Socrates had accused Euthyphro of being a Daedalus figure who caused arguments not to stay in the same place. Socrates now says ironically that Euthyphro's art leaves Daedalus in the dust, since Euthyphro makes an argument walk away and come back to the same spot (εἰς ταὐτόν, 15b11).

15b10   **κύκλῳ περιιόντα:** "going around in a circle." κύκλῳ is adverbial.

15c8   **οὐ καλῶς ὡμολογοῦμεν:** "we didn't agree beautifully"; that is, "we were wrong to agree."

15c9   **τιθέμεθα:** "assume." See also ὑποθέμενος (11c2), ὑποθέσεις (11c4), and προθώμεθα (11b7).

15c11–end   The conversation has come full circle. Socrates now seems to have been justified in his earlier surprise at Euthyphro's confidence regarding his understanding of τὰ θεῖα (4e) and τὸ ὅσιον. That coming to a defensible idea about τὸ ὅσιον will require a new approach should not surprise us. Socrates indicates at various points that he is not altogether satisfied with the way the conversation is going, with its missed opportunities (see comm. on 14c1–c2) and reliance on dubious stories about fighting among the gods (see comm. on 7b2).

15c12   **ἀποδειλιάσω:** Socrates will continue to investigate steadfastly. He will not slink away like a cowardly soldier. The comparison with bravery is

significant for Socrates' philosophical life. See *Ap.* 28e–29a, where he recalls
his willingness to obey the orders his civilian commanders gave (ἔταττον) at
Delium and Amphipolis and suggests a parallel between that behavior and his
determination to follow his understanding of the divinely inspired Delphic
oracle about him (τοῦ δὲ θεοῦ τάττοντος . . . φιλοσοφοῦντά με δεῖν ζῆν).
Socrates attempts to reorient the values of his fellow Athenians to show that
the stoic endurance of the philosopher is as valuable as that of the soldier. See
also *Rep.* 374e11, where the task of delineating the qualities of the guardians
is presumed to be difficult and to require persistence from Socrates and his
interlocutors (οὐκ ἀποδειλιατίον). At *Grg.* 480c5 Socrates affirms that a man
ought to submit to philosophical treatment like a medical patient, without
flinching (μὴ ἀποδειλιᾶν). **ἑκὼν εἶναι:** "willingly." For the absolute infinitive
construction, see Smyth 1956, 2012c.

15d1   **ἀτιμάσῃς:** Socrates continues to speak ironically, as if Euthyphro's
failure to disclose the nature of τὸ ὅσιον represented not his intellectual
laziness but a justified sense of superiority that could be understood as
scorning or otherwise dishonoring Socrates.

15d2–d3   **οἶσθα γὰρ εἴπερ τις ἄλλος ἀνθρώπων:** This type of faint praise
is typical of what Socrates says about questions he feels are unanswerable or
badly formed. See, for example, the discussion of his reaction on learning
that the sophist Evenus taught a course about *arete* at a price of five minas:
ἐμακάρισα εἰ ὡς ἀληθῶς ἔχοι ταύτην τὴν τέχνην, "I marveled if truly he had
that art" (*Ap.* 20c). The implication is that Evenus probably did not.

15d3   **οὐκ ἀφετέος εἶ:** "you must not be dismissed." ἀφετέος is a verbal
adjective < ἀφίημι, a verb that figures importantly in the dialogue. At 5b6,
Socrates imagines Meletus dismissing him from the lawsuit (ἀφίῃ) and
prosecuting Euthyphro (his "teacher") instead. See also 9c9, where Socrates
releases (ἀφίημι) Euthyphro from defending the apparent paradox that what is
loved by the gods is also hated by them.

In this passage, however, Socrates cannot in good conscience release
Euthyphro from the conversation. Socrates has no great expectation from
Euthyphro by now, but if Socrates can spur him to abandon his intellectual
laziness and self-satisfaction, Euthyphro could still exert himself in the future.
Such a discussion may not have been in vain.

It is useful here to compare *Phd.* 89b–c, where Socrates initially confuses
his interlocutors by suggesting that Phaedo will cut his hair as an act of
mourning Socrates after the execution is carried out, then reveals that not his
death but the death of philosophical conversation (*logos*) should cause them
to mourn. He proceeds to lift their spirits and encourage them to resume their

philosophical efforts. In *Euthyphro* also, even after much disappointment and without much trust in the willingness and ability of Euthyphro to stick it out, Socrates will not give up. He gives Euthyphro a final opportunity to abandon a life characterized by sloppy thought and self-delusion. **Πρωτεύς:** The allusion is to book 4 of the *Odyssey*. Menelaus recalls that when advised to seek knowledge about his return from Proteus, he was warned of Proteus' ability to assume a variety of forms: πάντα δὲ γινόμενος πειρήσεται, ὅσσ᾽ ἐπὶ γαῖαν/ ἑρπετὰ γίνονται καὶ ὕδωρ καὶ θεσπιδαὲς πῦρ, "He will attempt to become as many things as there are upon the earth and water and burning flame" (4.417–18). To subdue the god, Menelaus must hold him tightly: ἀστεμφέως ἐχέμεν μᾶλλόν τε πιέζειν (4.419). Only then will he give up his wisdom. Socrates portrays Euthyphro as a latter-day Proteus who will give up his wisdom only when compelled. Comparison with Proteus also makes good on the need for the different joke (ἄλλου . . . τινος . . . σκώμματος) to explain the inability of Euthyphro's arguments to stay in the same place (11c5). Instead of Daedalus, whom he was said to resemble, Euthyphro is now the ever-shifting Proteus, who must be held securely (οὐκ ἀφετέος εἶ) to make him give up what he claims to know.

15d4–d8   **εἰ γὰρ μὴ ᾔδησθα σαφῶς . . . ᾐσχύνθης:** Socrates summarizes ironically the high stakes that must have led Euthyphro to be absolutely sure he knew what he was doing in prosecuting his father (cf. 4e): Euthyphro must know τὸ ὅσιον since he has undertaken a prosecution that depended on a clear and accurate knowledge of it. Socrates identifies three factors that would have discouraged Euthyphro from taking the course that he has: (1) Euthyphro's indirect relationship with the low-status *pelates*, as opposed to the direct one with his father; (2) the possibility of incurring divine wrath (τοὺς θεοὺς ἂν ἔδεισας); and (3) the disapproval from humans that would certainly accompany Euthyphro's actions (τοὺς ἀνθρώπους ᾐσχύνθης).

15d5   **οὐκ ἔστιν ὅπως:** "there is no way that." For this formula introducing a counterfactual, see Isoc. 12.269.4. At *Ap.* 27e3 it is also used to pretend ironically that something that has actually happened is, in fact, impossible.

15d8   **ποιήσοις:** The future optative within a clause of fearing is used occasionally after past tenses to express a fear. See Goodwin 1890, 128, 131. **τοὺς ἀνθρώπους ᾐσχύνθης:** "feel shame before men."

15e1   **οἴει:** As Adam (1890, 106) notes, the qualification latent in "You think you know" is emphasized particularly here. The same word is used in Socrates' incredulous question at 4e5.

15e3   σπεύδω: Clearly a pretext on Euthyphro's part, since nothing has been said previously about his busy schedule. Elsewhere in the dialogue, he would have been eager to speak at length about the gods (6c). Euthyphro's εἰς αὖθις (some other time) picks up on Socrates' use of the same phrase to rein in Euthyphro at 6c8.

15e5   οἷα ποιεῖς: Exclamatory: "What a thing you are doing!" ἀπ᾽ ἐλπίδος . . . μεγάλης: Socrates metaphorically represents his hope for enlightenment as a height from which Euthyphro has cast him down by being unwilling to continue the conversation.

16a1   ἀπαλλάξομαι: "I will be freed from the charge." Socrates alludes to the fantasy that his instruction from Euthyphro will allow him to compel Meletus to abandon the prosecution (5a–b).

16a2   τὰ θεῖα: dependent on σοφός: "wise in respect to divine matters" (thus not the sort of man to commit *asebeia* again).

16a3   αὐτοσχεδιάζω: "speak offhandedly." See also comm. on 5a7 (αὐτοσχεδιάζοντα). Both instances describe what Socrates takes to be Meletus' opinion about Socrates' behavior.

16a4   καινοτομῶ: For the metaphor, see comm. on 3b6. ὅτι: Supply ἐνδειξάμενος.

Bibliography

Adam, J. 1890. *Platonis Euthyphro*. Cambridge: Cambridge University Press.

Asheri, David, Alan Lloyd, and Aldo Corcella. 2007. *A Commentary on Herodotus, Books I–IV*. Edited by Oswyn Murray and Alfonso Moreno. Oxford: Oxford University Press.

Baltes, Matthias. 1993. "Plato's School, the Academy." *Hermathena* 155:5–26.

Barber, E. J. W. 1992. "The Peplos of Athena." In *Goddess and Polis: The Panathenaic Festival in Ancient Athens*, edited by Jennifer Neils, 103–18. Princeton: Princeton University Press.

Biles, Gregory, and S. Douglas Olson, eds. 2016. *Aristophanes: "Wasps."* Oxford: Oxford University Press.

Bloch, Herbert. 1957. "The Exegetes at Athens: A Reply." *HSCP* 62:37–49.

Bluck, R. S. 1961. *Plato's "Meno."* Edited, with an introduction. Cambridge: Cambridge University Press.

Burkert, Walter. 1985. *Greek Religion: Archaic and Classical*. Translated by John Raffan. Cambridge, MA: Harvard University Press.

Burnet, John, ed. 1924. *Plato: "Euthyphro," "Apology of Socrates," "Crito."* Oxford: Clarendon.

Burnyeat, Myles, and Michael Frede. 2015. *The Pseudo-Platonic "Seventh Letter."* Edited by Domenic Scott. Cambridge: Cambridge University Press.

Bussanich, John, and Nicholas D. Smith, eds. 2013. *The Bloomsbury Companion to Socrates*. London: Bloomsbury.

Cairns, Douglas L. 1993. *Aidōs: The Psychology and Ethics of Honour and Shame in Ancient Greek Literature*. Oxford: Clarendon.

Carawan, Edwin. 2013. *The Athenian Amnesty and Reconstructing the Law*. Oxford: Oxford University Press.

Cohen, David. 1991. *Law, Sexuality, and Society: The Enforcement of Morals in Classical Athens*. Cambridge: Cambridge University Press.

Currie, Bruno. 2015. "Cypria." In *The Greek Epic Cycle and Its Ancient Reception: A Companion*. Edited by Marco Fantuzzi and Christos Tsagalis. Cambridge: Cambridge University Press.

d'Angour, Armand. 2011. *The Greeks and the New: Novelty in the Ancient Greek Imagination and Experience*. Cambridge: Cambridge University Press.

Davies, J. K. 1971. *Athenian Propertied Families, 600–300 B.C.* Oxford: Clarendon.

Denniston. J. D. 1934. *The Greek Particles.* Oxford: Clarendon.

Dodds, E. R., ed. 1990. *Plato: "Gorgias."* Oxford: Clarendon.

Dougherty, Caroline, and Leslie Kurke, eds. 1993. *Cultural Poetics in Archaic Greece.* Cambridge: Cambridge University Press.

Dover, K. J., ed. 1968. *Aristophanes: "Clouds."* Oxford: Clarendon.

Dover, K. J. 1994. *Greek Popular Morality in the Time of Plato and Aristotle.* Indianapolis: Hackett.

Duke, E. A., et al., eds. 1995. *Platonis Opera.* Vol. 1. Oxford: Clarendon.

Fantuzzi, Marco, and Christos Tsagalis. 2015. *The Greek Epic Cycle and Its Ancient Reception: A Companion.* Cambridge: Cambridge University Press.

Forbes, Clarence A. 1945. "Uses of the Greek Gymnasium." *CP* 40:32–42.

Gantz, Timothy. 1993. *Early Greek Myth: A Guide to Literary and Artistic Sources.* Baltimore: Johns Hopkins University Press.

Graves, C. E. 1881. *The "Euthyphro" and "Menexenus" of Plato.* London: MacMillan.

Greene, Guilielmus Chase, and Levi Arnold Post, eds. 1938. *Scholia Platonica.* Atlanta: Scholars Press.

Guthrie, W. K. C. 1975. *Plato: The Man and His Dialogues: Earlier Period.* Cambridge: Cambridge University Press.

Guthrie, W. K. C. 1978. *Plato: The Later Plato and the Academy.* Cambridge: Cambridge University Press.

Harrison, Alick Robin. 1998. *The Law of Athens.* Vol. 2. Indianapolis: Hackett.

Janko, Richard, ed. 1994. *The "Iliad": A Commentary.* Vol. 4, *Books 13–16.* Cambridge: Cambridge University Press.

Kahn, Charles. 1997. "Was Euthyphro the Author of the Derveni Papyrus?" In *Studies on the Derveni Papyrus,* edited by André Laks and Glen W. Most, 55–63. Oxford: Oxford University Press.

Kametkar, Rachana, ed. 2005. *Plato's "Euthyphro," "Apology," and "Crito": Critical Essays.* Lanham, MD: Roman and Littlefield.

Kirchner, Johannes. 1901–3. *Prosopographia Attica.* Vols. 1–2. Berlin: George Reimer.

Kirk, G. S., J. E. Raven, and M. Schofield. 1983. *The Presocratic Philosophers: A Critical History with a Selection of Texts.* Cambridge: Cambridge University Press.

Kraut, Richard. 2017. "Plato." In *The Stanford Encyclopedia of Philosophy,* Fall edition, edited by Edward N. Zalta. https://plato.stanford.edu/archives/fall2017/entries/plato/

Laks, André, and Glenn W. Most. 1997. *Studies on the Derveni Papyrus.* Oxford: Oxford University Press.

Ledger, Gerard. 1990. *Recounting Plato: A Computer Analysis of Plato's Style.* Oxford: Oxford University Press.

Lee, Jonathan, and Stephen Fineburg. 1982. "A Commentary on Plato's *Euthyphro*." Unpublished manuscript.

MacDowell, Douglas M. 1962. *Andocides: "On the Mysteries."* Oxford: Clarendon.

MacDowell, Douglas M. 1978. *The Law in Classical Athens.* Ithaca: Cornell University Press.

Marchent, E. C., and O. J. Todd, trans. 2013. *Xenophon: "Memorabilia," "Oeconomicus," "Symposium," "Apology."* Revised by Jeffrey Henderson. Loeb Classical Library 168. Cambridge, MA: Harvard University Press.

Martin, Richard. 1993. "The Seven Sages as Performers of Wisdom." In *Cultural Poetics of Archaic Greece*, edited by C. Dougherty and L. Kurke, 108–28. Cambridge: Cambridge University Press.

Mikalson, Jon D. 1983. *Athenian Popular Religion.* Chapel Hill: University of North Carolina Press.

Miller, P. A., and Charles Platter. 2010. *Plato's "Apology of Socrates": A Commentary.* Norman: University of Oklahoma Press.

Nails, Debra. 2002. *The People of Plato: A Prosopography of Plato and Other Socratics.* Indianapolis: Hackett.

Neils, Jennifer, ed. 1992. *Goddess and Polis: The Panathenaic Festival in Ancient Athens.* Princeton: Princeton University Press.

Parker, Robert. 1983. *Miasma: Pollution and Purification in Early Greek Religion.* Oxford: Clarendon.

Parker, Robert. 1996. *Athenian Religion: A History.* Oxford: Clarendon.

Phillips, David D. 2013. *The Law of Ancient Athens.* Ann Arbor: University of Michigan Press.

Poster, Carol. 1998. "The Idea(s) of Order of Platonic Dialogues and Their Hermeneutic Consequences." *Phoenix* 52:282–98.

Ralkowski, Mark. 2013. "The Politics of Impiety: Why Was Socrates Prosecuted by the Athenian Democracy?" In *The Bloomsbury Companion to Socrates*, edited by John Bussanich and Nicholas D. Smith, 301–27. London: Bloomsbury.

Rhodes, P. J. 1981. *A Commentary on the Aristotelian "Athenaion Politeia."* Oxford: Clarendon.

Rhodes, P.J. and Robin Osbourne. 2003.*Greek Historical Inscriptions 404-323 B.C.* Oxford: Oxford University Press.

Riginos, Alice. 1976. *Platonica: The Anecdotes concerning the Life and Writings of Plato.* Leiden: Brill.

Schiedel, Walter, and Elijah Meeks. Scheidel, W. and Meeks, E. (May 2, 2012). ORBIS: The Stanford Geospatial Network Model of the Roman World. Retrieved 11 Mar. 2019, from http://orbis.stanford.edu

Smyth, Herbert Weir. 1956. *Greek Grammar.* Revised by Gordon Messing. Cambridge, MA: Harvard University Press.

Strauss, Barry. 1993. *Fathers and Sons in Athens: Ideology and Society in the Era of the Peloponnesian War.* Princeton: Princeton University Press.

Strauss, Leo. 1966 *The City and Man*. Chicago: University of Chicago Press.

Strycker, Emile, and S. R. Slings. 1994. *Plato's "Apology of Socrates": A Literary and Philosophical Study with a Running Commentary*. Leiden: Brill.

Tell, Håkan. 2007. "Sages at the Games: Intellectual Displays and Dissemination of Wisdom in Ancient Greece." *Classical Antiquity* 26:249–75.

Tod, M. N. 1948. *A Selection of Greek Historical Inscriptions to the End of the Fifth Century B.C.* Vol. 2, *From 403 to 323 B.C.* Oxford: Clarendon.

Travlos, John. 1971. *Pictorial Dictionary of Ancient Athens*. New York: Praeger.

Leutsch, Ernst von, and Friedrich Schneidewin. 1839. *Corpus Paramoigraphorum Graecorum*. Vols. 1–2. Göttingen: Vandenhoeck und Ruprecht.

Watts, Edward. 2007. "Creating the Academy: Historical Discourse and the Shape of Community in the Old Academy." *Journal of Hellenic Studies* 127:6–22.

West, M. L., ed. 1964. *Hesiod: "Theogony."* Oxford: Oxford University Press.

Willi, Andreas. 1993. *The Languages of Aristophanes: Aspects of Linguistic Variation in Classical Attic Greek*. Oxford: Oxford University Press.

Woodruff, Paul. 2016. "Plato's Shorter Ethical Works." In *The Stanford Encyclopedia of Philosophy*, Winter edition, edited by Edward N. Zalta. https://plato.stanford.edu/archives/win2016/entries/plato-ethics-shorter/

Index

Made in the
USA
Middletown, DE